Stop It, Mom!!

7 Powerful Methods to Overcome and Recover from a Narcissistic Mother

By C Moffett

Table of Contents

Conclusion

References

Introduction

*" **The best way out is always through.** "*

*—**Robert Frost***

The words came out of his mouth like blades, piercing into my entire being. I couldn't see any blood coming out, but felt the wounds opening up, yet again. The rattling of the dishes as I washed them, mixed with the bickering made me feel like I've always been on the wrong side of the argument. Was it the first time this happened? No. Every time I tried to express my needs, every time I called him out on his horrendous behavior, he would go to every possible length, just to prove himself right. My husband wasn't good at handling criticism. It felt like I was constantly walking on eggshells. Attempting to do something for me was a challenge. All I did was inform him that I had gotten a job.

"You can't manage the home and office simultaneously, I think you should reconsider."

Was I bothered? I've observed this cycle of patterns so many times, that I couldn't care less. He was a good man. The reflection of the past I saw in him, made me question all the love I had for him. All these years I was being guilt-tripped for taking care of myself. None of my achievements, or my efforts, were ever appreciated. I was made to feel that If I become my authentic self, people will be bothered. Was I being selfish? No, because as soon as you gain awareness of your self-worth, some people around you might get affected.

"Never be bullied into silence. Never allow yourself to be made a victim. Accept no one's definition of your life; define yourself."
— Harvey Fierstein

Have you ever felt like speaking up for yourself causes hurdles for you?
Do you sometimes think that you do not have a hold over your life?
Are you constantly put down by controlling behavior?

If so, you are not alone. I have encountered such challenging thoughts and emotions myself. It might feel like you are going in circles, hoping that one day you'll find a way out. Trust that there is always a new way to look at things. I was caught up in the rabbit role for so long that I could not recognize the damage it was causing me. But when I did, it was unbelievable. The circumstances around us are truly a reflection of our inner workings. How you feel inside is how you perceive the environment.

These questions are very basic, compared to what is hidden behind closed doors. The effects, and the consequences, require a broader stance. If you are experiencing excruciating thoughts regarding any of these traits, the reason behind them might be the presence of a narcissistic person in your life.

First, let's talk about the facts. Or should I call them *"Red Flags?"*

To a certain degree, we all possess narcissistic traits. If we feel like we are in some kind of threat or being mistreated, our initial response is self-defense. This response comes from our ego, which we all possess. There is a healthy ego, and then there exists its toxic side. Narcissism is a trait that can even drain an empath dry. You will feel like a narcissist has this wool wrapped over your eyes, blinding the vision.

This is just the tip of the iceberg. I can relate to the narcissistic dynamic quite well. Why me, you might be wondering. It is because I have dealt with narcissistic parents. Of course, I was not aware of this until I grew up to find out how I have encumbered those traits as well. My friendships were toxic, relationships were chaotic, and my sense of being was shattered.

Constantly being controlled, questioned, and dominated by my parents.

These wounds bled into other regions of my life. I started noticing the red flags in my teenage years but was not sure what to make of it. It took me 30 long years to understand the depth of the suffering. Being aware of the red flags is not the only thing that helped me. The long therapy sessions I had, as well as coaching classes were like stepping stones in my healing process. It took a long time to heal my wounds but it was worth it. I've now become a mental health counselor myself. I educate people through social platforms on how to heal the trauma bonds created by narcissistic parents.

If you are struggling with self-esteem issues, dealing with a narcissistic person or encountering relationship problems, this book will be your ultimate guideline. The problem for me was domination and manipulation by my mother.

And my father, that is another addition to the existing trauma.

"Will I ever be good enough?" For yourself? Always. For a narcissist? Never!

Does this thought pop into your mind often? Have you ever been called crazy just because you stood up for yourself? If so, this book will provide you with solutions that can heal your inner child. Because I have witnessed the firsthand social impact of these behaviors, I want to shed light on the fact that you can overcome them. Heal the trauma, instead of just sweeping the fears and concerns under the rug, as it has always been done, historically. I feel like I have experienced more than enough to have a valuable perspective that allows me to elucidate the trials and tribulations of having a narcissistic mother.

"Narcissistic personality disorder is named for Narcissus, from Greek mythology, who fell in love with his reflection. Freud used the term to describe self-absorbed persons, and

psychoanalysts have focused on the narcissist's need to bolster his or her self-esteem through grandiose fantasy, exaggerated ambition, exhibitionism, and feelings of entitlement."

— **Donald W. Black**

It is tough being around, and under, the influence of a narcissist. If you aren't aware of this disorder, and its traits, you'll probably fall victim to this. Nobody in the right state of mind will want to see their life falling apart. Especially because of other people.

We are thriving each day, striving to be the best iteration of who we were intended to be. Growing. Who doesn't want to improve themselves? You can always choose to be happy, and let nothing hold you back.

So, what are we going to learn from this book?
How to heal from a narcissist.

Can we break the shackles that hold us back? Absolutely! But only if we know how their calculated tactics, to manipulate you, work.

First and foremost, this book highlights the problems encountered by individuals who have experienced abuse.

How do these problems affect their relationships, and the arduous attempts to find their real selves? The most important concern of people, who are abused by narcissistic people, is "How to spot them"? Believe it or not, it's hard to spot a narcissist most of the time, especially if you are an empath.

"People are afraid to heal because their entire identity is centered around the trauma they've experienced. They have no idea who they are outside of trauma and that unknown is terrifying."

— Ebonee Davis

It is significant to understand the long-term effects of mental abuse caused by narcissists. Yes, it takes time to heal these wounds, but then again, it's never too late. In this book, we are going to unravel the secrets of an egocentric personality.

Let us embark on this healing journey together and create a happy, satisfied and productive version of ourselves. Shall we?

Chapter 1

Is there a problem?

Have you ever come across people who think that they don't have a problem?

While they are the epitome of the problem. Or someone who needs to be admired all the time? People who need to be the center of attention and apathetic about others' emotions. We should know that all of us possess narcissistic tendencies. Narcissism can be identified as a personality trait as well as a personality disorder. Both are remarkably different from each other. If we talk about the disorder itself, it has only one type. This is, of course, a mental disorder that is usually diagnosed when narcissism protracts beyond a personality trait. It affects many areas of life constantly. There are mainly two types that help us differentiate the fruitful, and harmful, aspects of narcissism:

- **Adaptive Narcissism**

This type of narcissism refers to the traits which can be productive for an individual. Such as high confidence, self-reliance and the ability to celebrate oneself. But for some people, adaptive narcissism can turn into something very unhealthy. Do you know who we are talking about? A narcissist! People who are seen as overestimating their abilities with the habit of trying to control and manipulate others. A narcissist will portray themselves in such a way that others will see them as someone flawless. Adaptive narcissism is also known as grandiose narcissism. In this type of narcissism, a person may see themselves as being better than others. A narcissist with an adaptive type may hide under their successes and are usually very charming. They appear to be quite friendly and welcoming and might possess great leadership qualities.

- **Maladaptive Narcissism**

The traits which are unhealthy and toxic fall into this category. Such as controlling behavior, aggression, a sense of entitlement, and taking advantage of others. These are the traits associated with Narcissistic Personality Disorder.

Usually, when talking about narcissists, the traits mentioned in the maladaptive type are the ones that should be considered. However, this is only a one-dimensional side of narcissistic personality disorder. Let's talk in-depth about the different types of narcissism that exist in your life:

- **Overt narcissism**

Have you ever had a friend who is always babbling about their successes? I did this and I did that. I'm so good at this! No one could achieve this as I did and so on. Overt narcissism can be described using several words including grandiose narcissism and agentic narcissism. Most people can relate to this kind because these toxic personality traits are evident in people around them. These traits are associated with a narcissistic personality disorder.

Some of the characteristics of an overt narcissist include:
- *Arrogance*
- *Outgoing*
- *Overbearing*
- *Entitled*
- *Exaggerated outlook on self*
- *A constant need for admiration and praise*
- *Lack of empathy*
- *Exploitative*
- *Competitive*

People like these usually lack empathy and don't experience emotions like sadness or loneliness. They can be seen boasting about almost everything they do.

Basically, the "know it all" kind of person. They feel like no one could ever match their level of intelligence.

When speaking to a particular friend of mine, the second I tell her about anything I've achieved, she starts rambling about her own so-called exaggerated accomplishments. She can make a chicken look like an elephant, due to the charisma in her tone. She thinks I can't see through her lies, but I certainly can. I act as if I believe them out of consideration, so she keeps on going...amazingly confident. While this kind can sometimes be spotted easily, there is another kind of narcissism that tends to stay under the sheets.

- **Covert Narcissism**

Unlike overt narcissists, covert narcissists do not display the usual traits of narcissistic personality disorder, which are arrogance and a sense of entitlement. Overt narcissists display low self-esteem and insecurity. From my experience, it is always hard to spot a covert narcissist. I have dealt with this kind of narcissist several times, and it felt like I was going crazy.

Some traits of people with covert narcissism include:
- *Insecurity*

- *Low self-confidence*
- *More prone to other mental disorders such as anxiety, depression, and shame*
- *Defensiveness*
- *Avoidant behavior*
- *Tendency to play the victim*

For someone with covert narcissism, it is very difficult to accept criticism. Whenever they do hear any form of criticism, they tend to act defensively. Whether they are wrong or right, they are the only ones who are suffering.

- **Antagonistic Narcissism**

According to some research, antagonistic narcissism is derived from overt narcissism. The main traits that are highlighted are rivalry and competition. Other traits include:

- Arrogance
- Prone to arguing
- Tendency to compete with others
- Taking advantage of others

Some researchers have discovered that people with this type of narcissism have a hard time trusting others. It was also revealed that it's hard for them to forgive people as well.

- **Communal Narcissism**

This is also a subtype of overt narcissism, where a person might be seen as altruistic and very helpful towards others. However, in actuality, the opposite is the case. The ironic part is that narcissists are bothered because of social injustices, but their mistreatment towards others does not affect them at all.

- **Malignant Narcissism**

This type is closely linked to overt narcissism. People with this sub-type of narcissism are highly abusive and can do everything to hurt others and gain their benefit. They possess anti-social traits and are usually sadistic. They lack empathy for others. This is one severe kind of narcissism and the person having this type can harm themselves as well. People afflicted with Malignant narcissism are generally:

- Sadistic
- Aggressive
- Vindictive
- Suffer from paranoia

This type of narcissism is the worst kind because people with malignant narcissism can cause havoc in your life. They are always wearing a mask and everything is a facade. You never know their true selves nor do they reveal it. They feel like they are under some kind of threat and often play the victim. They may even go as far as to harass people just for their enjoyment.

Have you ever felt as though, no matter how hard you try, there are some people you never seem to get along with?
People, who are so engrossed in their arrogance that nothing else matters to them?

These are the kind of people who are identified as narcissists. People who can manipulate you into thinking and doing anything. If you feel like there is someone around you that is defensive and does not appreciate criticism, you're probably dealing with type of narcissist!

Living with a narcissist is endless mental abuse. If you are accustomed to manipulation and feel like there's something wrong with you, there isn't. Because narcissists are so good at manipulation, it's difficult to identify their real side. On the downside, they leave a trail of patterns that signifies the traits they carry.

How about we have a look into the fantasy land narcissists live in?

- **The Sense of Entitlement**

This is one of the most significant aspects of narcissistic people. Narcissists feel like the whole world should revolve around them. They always want to feel like the center of attention and they possess a sense of entitlement.

Have you ever come across someone who's ego touches the sky? Someone who disregards others suffering?

Everything must be a certain way for them. If they feel like anything is heading south, they will likely rant and start complaining. They deserve all the good and the suffering is just some bad luck, they don't deserve. They feel like they are the alphas who deserve the best of the best. No harm should come to them and no calamity shall befall them. Because they feel so entitled, they always tend to consider themselves better than others.

- **The expectation for Admiration**

Ever seen people who want to be admired so much that they start praising themselves?

With narcissists, the need for admiration holds great value. It is because they are so conscious about their image, the constant praise is what keeps them alive. I question myself sometimes about how much admiration a narcissist requires to feel satisfied. The answer is never enough. Accepting criticism is a big no for such people. Narcissists expect to be admired. If their expectations are not being met, they will likely get infuriated over it.

- **Superiority Complex**

Most narcissists tend to see themselves as superior to others. They feel that there is no one like them. It is good to have confidence in oneself, but boasting about one's attributes every chance they get is inappropriate, to say the least. If anyone tries to criticize a narcissist, they will probably get aggressive and instead, start finding fault in others. Narcissists are often seen insulting the waiters or people working for them. They may ridicule people they think are below them, especially support staff or hospitality workers. Does it make you feel sick to the stomach? If they are faced with a challenging situation, they tend to criticize the world around them. Their ego is always brimming with negativity, which is what makes them think they are superior to other people.

- **Exaggeration**

One of my uncles has a tendency of making the most common experiences of his life look like it's an action movie. He comes up with stories that feel otherworldly. A world that doesn't exist.

With narcissists, it is common to lie about things that do not require dishonesty or exaggeration, but they are compelled to do it. If you are smart or lucky enough, you will pick up on it early, and then sit back and enjoy the story – perhaps die laughing inside. They keep on exaggerating their life to impress other people. Their lives spiral around the tiny successes they have obtained, and they will continue to babble about them all the time. If a narcissist gets confronted about a lie they told, they will likely make up an additional story about that as well. The consistent exaggeration is what tells us how delusional a narcissistic person can be.

- **Need to Take Control**

Narcissists take the time to analyze each person they encounter in their lives. They are extremely manipulative and can manage each person according to the said person's emotions/weak points.

The sense of entitlement they possess makes them want to take charge of everything and it must be according to their plan. If a certain expectation of a narcissist is not met, they will probably throw a tantrum. They make plans so tactfully and logically, that a normal person can easily fall prey to them. For narcissists, other people are like puppets, who they like to control all the time.

Have you ever felt dominated by someone in your life?

- **Lack of empathy**

Generally speaking, narcissists don't care about others. They are blind to how others feel and how they act. Everything that matters to them is how they see the world and their perspective on things. They are a threat to other people as well as themselves. Vulnerable people are more prone to being exploited by a narcissist. They are not able to see other people's perspectives or their sufferings. All they care about is themselves, and how everything should function according to their wants and needs. They are not able to understand even the most basic emotions like happiness and peace.

Have you come across a person who you believed was indifferent toward any emotion?

- **Fantasy World**

There is nothing in this world that plays out the way we think. The narcissists live in their dream world where everything must be a certain way. Their superego lets them see the world however they perceive it to be.

How delusional is that?

How a narcissist views the world is grand, while the reality oftentimes is quite opposite. They tend to ignore the harsh truths of life. If anyone tries to invade their fantasy land, a narcissist would act defensively and violently. Because they lived in guilt and shame all their lives, living in a fantasy world works like a defense mechanism for them. If a narcissist were able to get out of their dreamland, there is no way they would be able to survive.

- **Interrupting others**

When you come face to face with a narcissist, you might notice that they tend to interrupt a lot, in any conversation. This is because generally, it doesn't really matter what the other person has to say. They tend to be impatient when they have to listen to others and might interrupt the conversation grotesquely. Have you every had a conversation with someone that asks a question, and before you even have a chance to answer, they are already thinking about the next question they want to ask? Or one worse, they will ask you a question, and then start to answer it for you, as if your opinion or answer is predetermined and you don't *really* have anything to contribute to the conversation.

If they feel like another person is gaining some sort of attention, they'll probably revert the topic to themselves. A narcissistic person might cut off a conversation like they're going to present a new way to eliminate the injustices in the world, but you know what they'll say instead? The only thing that matters for a narcissist is their point of view. All they seek is attention and will do and say anything to gain it.

I washed the clothes without a washing machine today! Oh, what an effort it was, I bet no one can wash clothes like this.

- **Lack of accountability and Blaming Others**

There is nothing wrong with a narcissist (in their mind). Anything they do, anything they say, is always accurate and no one should dare criticize it. They feel the need to control everything when something does not work according to their narcissist textbook; easier to blame others. There is no way a narcissistic person will ever own up to their mistake. When things aren't perfect, they guilt trip others and don't take responsibility for their mistakes. When you try to call out a narcissist for their foolish behavior, they will come up with excuses and lies to let it all fall on you. They will manipulate you into thinking you are the one who is exaggerating the situation, and there's nothing wrong with them. Instead of a simple apology for their drunken outburst, I had one former friend simply state that they "...own their (crazy) behaviour" and you just have to accept it or get out. I chose to get out.

This is because of the sense of entitlement they feel for themselves. They consider themselves so perfect that others are seen as utterly flawed. And even if they have a single flaw, they are so perfect elsewise that you should just get over it. Narcissists tend to blame the people they are close with, the most. The mistakes a narcissist makes are transferred as a burden onto other people's shoulders.

- **The desire for Perfection**

Ever seen a human without flaws? Ever seen someone who does *not* make mistakes? Yes! A narcissist. Their desire for perfection seems superfluous. One can only be this perfect in a world that doesn't exist. Reality is entirely different from their perception. The narcissists deem themselves superhumans. Their expectations of life are far-fetched from how the real-world works. These high expectations are carried to all aspects of their life. Their relationships, workplaces and every part of their life have to be perfect. Even the events that take place in their life should unravel according to their curated timeline. Is that even possible? A narcissist lacks the mental skills to understand these basic notions and emotions. The desire for perfection costs them so much and yet, they don't recognize it.

- **Lack of Boundaries**

No matter how hard a narcissist plans about doing things or approaching a person, or a situation, they cannot possibly assume the outcome. They might try to manipulate a person and expect the same response over and over again. But what if the person decides to change the response? You will then see a narcissist's ego crushing under a rock. Their delusional mind makes them think they own everyone.

Everyone should feel and think like they want to, which is not possible at all. Instead, a narcissistic person will be outraged if you try to act or speak against their desires. This is a time when all their manipulation tactics come into play because they feel threatened by other people. If you try to cross a boundary, you will be subjected to mental abuse of all kinds. A narcissist knows no bounds and will do anything to hurt others. They are self-centered and show no empathy towards others.

- **Intimidation and Bullying**

So, what happens when you do not give in to a narcissist? When a narcissist feels like they have encountered someone better than them, they will usually tend to bully and demean them. They can use all kinds of brutal tactics just to get their way. If reality differs from the expected outcome, a narcissist will start to feel agitated.

"You made me do that!" is a common phrase a narcissist might use after bullying you!

Anyone submitting to narcissistic people is only feeding their ego. So long as a narcissist's ego remains intact, it is all good. A narcissist might feel threatened if they encounter another individual doing better than them. A narcissist will call out names, try to destroy your self-esteem, insult you and all this will be said scornfully. You will feel like you mean nothing to them, which is true in most cases. They might scare you with threats of abandonment or badger you endlessly.

- **Insecurities and Fears:**

Have you ever thought about why narcissists act the way they do? They carry deep-rooted fears and insecurities which reflect in their behavior and actions. They see themselves as a perfect human without any flaws. The thoughts they have, or the outlook they have about themselves, are because of the sense of entitlement attached to it. Narcissists are scared to peek inside themselves so they can't accept their flaws. The life of a narcissist is nothing less than drama. While everything might look perfect on the outside, they are miserable inside. They are terrified of abandonment and rejection, because of their past experiences with others.

- **Vulnerability**

Most narcissists lack emotional depth. Even if there is some, it is tactfully used to seek advantage from others. They will do anything to get their way, even if it means being emotionally responsive towards others for their benefit. However, you will not see them being vulnerable themselves. Because they are so analytical about everything, they fear being vulnerable. They are not able to express their emotions, which is one reason why they can even manipulate a therapist. Can you imagine? A professional therapist falling into the manipulation trap of a narcissist?

Vulnerability for a narcissist is merely a weakness that will lead to abandonment and pain from others. Emotional vulnerability is one of the reasons why relationships with narcissists become unbearable. Narcissists encounter serious problems expressing their emotions, which leads to unsuccessful relationships. As weird as it may sound, they do not like seeing vulnerability in others as well. If another person is trying to reveal their emotional side, a narcissist will get annoyed by the display and throw a temper tantrum and turn attention towards themselves.

- **Extraordinary Amount of Validation and Attention**

Narcissists thrive off other people's energy. If they are not being given the level of attention and validation expected, they become irritated. Being human, we do require validation as a sign that we are doing okay. But when this trait has no bounds, it becomes toxic. It is not that narcissists seek attention only from their closest relationships, they expect attention from everyone. Even the ones they barely know. Isn't that strange? They need all the support, validation and attention but ironically, they don't reciprocate. A normal person living with a narcissist may feel drained and burnt out most of the time, feeding their ego and unrealistic expectations.

- **Mesmerizing Personality**

Most narcissists have a personality that will leave you in awe. They are the people you love to hate...or hate to love. They are loud, charming and persuasive. They run a great business, but not you would like to work with one. One can give in easily to a narcissist because of the attractiveness and manipulation tactics.

This kind of personality makes a narcissist think that they can treat others like puppets, making them act according to their expectations. The people around narcissists suffer when they have to provide attention at the cost of their well-being. Narcissists tend to be very loving and passionate in the initial stages of a relationship, and afterward, all that is left is manipulation and mental abuse.

It is important to know that having confidence, and realizing one's self-worth, does not mean the individual is a narcissist. But when this confidence exceeds healthy levels, you know who and what you are dealing with.

"Mirror, mirror on the wall, who is the fairest of them all?"
"Me, obviously!"

When the super-sized ego comes in the way, you know you're dealing with a narcissist.
An alternative model of diagnosing personality disorders, such as NPD, was proposed in the DSM-V. This model is defined by four particular areas of functioning, in which, personality disorders are most likely to be located. There

are four more traits that should be considered to diagnose a person with narcissistic personality disorder (NPD). These are as follows:

- **Identity**

Narcissists usually suffer from an identity crisis. They do not know themselves. They have extreme expectations regarding how other people see them but not what they are inside. This happens to boost their self-esteem. They seem to be excessively worried about what others think of them, rather than what they think of themselves. Most of the time, the narcissist is seen applauding their success and victories. So other people might perceive a narcissist only on the surface level.

- **Self-direction**

Deeply immersed in their superiority complex, a narcissist may do anything to get their way. The sense of entitlement makes them feel that others are inferior to them. Sometimes this is coupled with the one-sided competition with others. A narcissist may feel like only they can achieve a certain goal, and nobody else.

- **Empathy**

Narcissists are extremely logical and practical. Most of them cannot relate to others' sufferings, as they can't walk a mile in someone else's shoes, even though they'll tell you that the have been there before and know exactly *it* is. A narcissist might show emotion according to the circumstances, or whenever they want to benefit from the situation. This is the very reason a narcissist is unable to connect with other people on an emotional level. No matter how hard you try, your emotions will not reach a narcissist.

- **Intimacy**

You won't find a single narcissist that has true friends or partners. Sadly, they lack any sort of emotional intelligence. The relationships a narcissist forms are as superficial as their fantasyland. They have high expectations from others, which leads to disruption within relationships. They lack the emotional skills to maintain healthy relationships. All relationships for them are like ego boosters without any emotional intimacy.

Causes of Narcissistic Personality Disorder

You might be wondering what causes *Narcissistic Personality Disorder*. To know why certain people function differently than us, we need to pull back the curtains. The brain functioning of narcissists is different from normal people. Some researchers found fewer amounts of gray matter in the left anterior insula. This part of the brain is responsible for cognitive functioning, emotional regulation, compassion, and empathy. According to Dr. Hallett, narcissistic traits do not evolve into personality disorders. Rather personality disorders are developed through childhood experiences, genetics, and the environment. These disorders are more likely to be diagnosed in the teenage years or older. According to scientists, there is no single cause of NPD, other interpersonal factors are responsible for diagnosing a full-blown disorder. Some of them include:

- Being born with an oversensitive temperament
- Learning manipulative behavior from parents or peers
- Being excessively praised for good behaviors
- Being excessively criticized for bad behaviors
- Suffering from severe childhood abuse or neglect
- Inconsistent or unpredictable parental caregiving
- Growing up with unrealistic expectations from parents
- Being excessively pampered or overindulged by parents, peers, or family members

- Being excessively admired with no real feedback to ground you with reality
- Receiving excessive praise from parents or others focused on your looks or abilities (Krista Soriano,2022)

"Hold yourself back, or heal yourself back together. You decide."

— *Brittany Burgunder*

Do you have C-PTSD?

Have you ever thought about the effects of mental abuse on an individual?

The prolonged mental abuse a person suffers at the hands of a narcissist creates deep-rooted trauma. Most people are not able to identify the fears that come from trauma. Have you ever noticed being anxious when you are around a narcissist? The reason you might feel this way is because you've been experiencing complex *post-traumatic stress disorder*, (C-PTSD or just PTSD). This is an anxiety condition involving symptoms of PTSD along with other symptoms. This condition is caused when someone has experienced trauma for prolonged periods. These traumatic events can be mental abuse, near-death experiences, natural disasters etc.

PTSD AND C-PTSD are similar but the symptoms of C-PTSD are more severe. The effects of both are similar, such as being anxious and fearful, insomnia, flashbacks, and nightmares. When it comes to the difference between both, C-PTSD usually results from prolonged mental abuse (since childhood), while PTSD is caused by a single traumatic event. The effect of C-PTSD lasts longer than PTSD and the consequences are severe, Herman, J. L. (1992). Some of the differences are as follows:

C-PTSD:
- Caused by long-term reiterated trauma
- Originates from childhood experiences
- Typically arises in those who have suffered oppression and racism
- More severe than PTSD.

PTSD:
- Caused by a singular traumatic event
- Milder than C-PTSD
- Can result from trauma experienced at any age

You might be experiencing symptoms of C-PTSD without even realizing its existence. Sometimes, when you're in the cycle of abuse, you forget who you are. This is the result of trauma. There are other symptoms which are involved in this disorder. Some of them include:

- **Difficulty controlling emotions.**

People with CPTSD are more likely prone to suicidal thoughts, depression, prolonged periods of sadness and extreme anger. This is because it is difficult for them to control their emotions and their reactions become explosive (Ford & Courtois, 2014).

- **Negative self-image.**

People with C-PTSD usually feel guilty, ashamed, and helpless. This disorder makes a person feel like they don't belong anywhere. They see themselves negatively most of the time (Giourou et al., 2018).

- **Difficult relationships.**

With C-PTSD, people usually get into difficult relationships because of what they've experienced in the past. They have difficulty trusting others and sometimes tend to avoid relationships as well (Lawson,2017).

- **Detachment from the trauma.**

Some people might forget their trauma but it exists deep within. They may try to disconnect themselves from the world around them. These self-defense mechanisms are known as depersonalization and derealization.

- **Loss of identity.**

The long periods of mental abuse can make a person forget their core beliefs, faith and values. Because of the violent experiences, they might lose hope in other people as well as the world around them.

These symptoms of C-PTSD are grave and may affect all areas of a person's life. This includes relationships, personal life, work, social interactions, and worldview. There are numerous reasons why you keep on questioning your self-worth.

"Traumatized people chronically feel unsafe inside their bodies: The past is alive in the form of gnawing interior discomfort. Their bodies are constantly bombarded by visceral warning signs, and, in an attempt to control these processes, they often become experts at ignoring their gut feelings and numbing awareness of what is played out inside. They learn to hide from their selves."

The negative consequences of living with mental abuse haunt us our entire lives. Most of the time, this abuse comes from our nearest and dearest relationships, our parents.

It is hard to talk about our parents in such a manner but when it comes to one's mental well-being, it's crucial to understand what influence our parents have on us. When we are able to identify whether we are living in a healthy or toxic environment, we can make better decisions for our life.

Do you feel like you always get into toxic relationships? Has it ever occurred that you are living a life under the influence of your parents?
Can you identify your authentic self, unhampered by others' influence?

If you're stuck in your head, feeling overwhelmed by such questions, know that you aren't insane to feel this way.

"When I was with my mother, I sometimes thought of myself as a trophy—something to be

*flaunted before friends. When out of public view,
I sat on the shelf ignored and forgotten."*

—Joan Frances Casey

Chapter:2

Not All Mothers Can Love

Childhood is the most precious time of a person's life. There are no worries, no sorrow and plenty of carefree time. A time when we are surrounded by the love and affection of our parents.

What was your childhood like? Was it carefree and happy or did you grow up before time?

During childhood years we learn a lot from our parents. Children will pick up their parent's behaviors, actions, ethics and sometimes their beliefs as well. It is the responsibility of parents to provide their children with adequate care. Both the mother and the father are responsible for the upbringing of their children. They are supposed to guide their children when they do something wrong. Because our parents play an important role in shaping our personality. That is one example of healthy parenting.

However, if you have lived under the roof of toxicity, your childhood has been significantly different. The parenting dynamic in a toxic household shatters the personality of the children. If the parents aren't aware of their flaws and act like kids themselves, how are they supposed to take care of the children?

I was ignored by my parents in my childhood, a time when I needed their love and attention the most. They were always fighting and bickering. It wasn't just about me, my other siblings were affected equally. My father used to spend most of his time focusing on his business, while my mother manipulated us in every way she could.
Everything I knew of myself was through her words. I saw myself as her reflection. How I perceived the world was from her eyes, not mine. These feelings are just a drop in the bucket.
If you can relate to my feelings, you're probably dealing with a narcissistic mother. If you are a daughter of a narcissistic mother, the healing journey might be a long one. But you must never lose hope.
If you feel like you want to heal your inner child, the first step is making yourself aware of the signs. Do you ever doubt yourself? Or feel like you are being controlled by your mother?

The following are some of the clues about a narcissistic mother that might heal your inner child:

- **Controlling**

Have you ever felt like your mother tends to neglect your decisions? It's because she wants you to act the way she wants. If you try to stand up for yourself, you'll probably be shunned by her.

"You should wear this instead; it'll look much better than what you chose!"
Meanwhile, I look like a clown.

She will make you feel guilty and ashamed of yourself if your opinions differ from hers. Narcissistic mothers want their children to meet her expectations. There's no concept of individuality for a narcissistic mother. She only wants you to serve her needs.

- **Unconditional Love**

Why wouldn't a mother want to see their children succeed? Every mother does, but a narcissistic mother has selfish reasons behind this as well. She wants to look and feel good about what you have achieved. She'll never truly appreciate you for what you've accomplished. And if you are, by chance, succeeding inordinately, a narcissistic mother might feel jealous. The daughters of such mothers tend to be perfectionists, just to achieve their mother's love.

- **She cannot tolerate your point of view**

There is no way a narcissistic mother would want to listen to what you have to say. If your perspective differs from hers, she will try to put you down. Even if she does listen, there is no acknowledgment on her part. She'll try to shame or guilt-trip you for having a different point of view. Here is a light-hearted example:

Me to my mother, "How about we cook pasta tonight?"
My mother ,"Are you going to pay for the expensive grocery" or "How about you cook it yourself?"

- **Unpredictable**

Have you encountered such a situation where you've opposed your mother, and instead of giving the usual toxic treatment, she *love-bombs* you? Narcissistic mothers tend to act this way when they need attention from you. It happens so that you do not feel negatively towards her. She would immediately try to protect her self-image by providing you with the love you need. You'll only receive care according to her needs, and when she's doing okay, the ignorance kicks in.

- **Constant manipulation**

Are you afraid to say no to your mother? Does her anger scare you? The reason why you feel this way is that you are being manipulated by a narcissistic mother. If you don't feel like doing something that she asks for, she might guilt trip or shame you. All of this is done so subtly, that you will end up doubting yourself. There will come a point, you will start believing the taunts and insults given by your mother.

- **No validation of feelings**

Do you remember a time when you were feeling emotional and thought of sharing it with your mother? How did she respond?

If you ever feel hurt by your narcissistic mother, and stand up to confront her, she will probably make it about herself. She will never validate your feelings, nor will she acknowledge them. Narcissistic mothers lack emotional consciousness; therefore, they cannot understand your feelings. She'll only be concerned about the criticism you imposed on her. The attention should only be on her.

- **Dominating**

Narcissists think they are above everyone else. The superiority complex and sense of entitlement a narcissist possesses make them think that no rules apply to them. The rules are only made for people below a narcissist, and people should follow the rules as well. I remember this incident from childhood when my mother was late for her dentist's appointment. It was her mistake and she could not get there on time.

Do you know what she did? Upon arriving, she caused havoc at the clinic, trying to break in on another patient. She blamed the dentist for assisting another person before her. She even threw a temper tantrum at me, in front of everyone. I felt embarrassed at that moment because of her impulsive behavior.

- **I care only about self-image**

Narcissists are heavily focused on their self-image. All they truly care about is how others perceive them, especially the ones whose opinions matter to them. Have you ever seen your mom act differently at home than she does at social gatherings? Have you ever felt like she's explosive at home and perfectly composed publicly? It's because narcissistic mothers want to appear excellent in front of others so it goes well with the image they've created for them. I would often meet my mother's coworkers or church friends, and they would always remark how lucky I must feel to be *her* daughter. I usually just smiled though the thoughts running through my head were, "are we still talking about the same lady?"

- **Humiliation**

A mother knows her child too well. She understands their emotions, needs and behavior. A narcissistic mother will almost always use this information negatively. She'll try to belittle you in front of others and will hit the spot where it hurts the most. She'll be judgemental and will condemn every move you make.

Did your mother ever try to humiliate you when you were feeling excited or happy? Saying, "*So this makes you all geared up, and when I ask you to clean the dishes, you make up excuses!*" She can never really see you enjoying or being happy on your own, can she?

- **Volatile**

Narcissists are emotionally inconsistent. Their temper rises from zero to a hundred within a matter of time. You never know when you have made the narcissist upset.

They can be cool and collected one minute and the next minute you will probably encounter an infuriated side. A narcissistic mother can be quite volatile with her emotions.

- **Boundaries**

Boundaries? What boundaries? There is no such thing in the book of a narcissist. Has there been a time in your life when you felt like someone trampled your boundaries? When it comes to healthy parenting, parents usually tend to give space to their children rather than interfering in all matters. They understand that not everything can be done according to their expectations. However, people with NPD feel challenged with this concept. They cannot take *no* for an answer. When it comes to a narcissistic mother, she will always get what she wants. No matter how high you build that wall, to her, it would be nothing.

- **Invisibility**

Have you ever felt like you were invisible to your parents? The most concerning part of a narcissistic dynamic is the lack of emotional availability from the parents. When the children's emotional needs are neglected, they tend to feel disoriented and isolated. It is the most basic need of a child, to be loved and understood by their parents.

Whenever I was upset and anxious about something, I always looked to my mother for support. Most of the time she would not listen, but when she did, her response was hurtful. She disregarded my emotions and thought I was exaggerating the situation.

- **Competition**

You would not see healthy parents compete with their children. Parents should always desire the best for us and always wish that we make the best of life. The global standard of parenting success is to have a child surpass your own success, financial status or degree of happiness. They always want us to have a better life than they did. Not surprising, this isn't the case when it comes to a narcissistic mother.

"Your boyfriend isn't as good as mine, he used to treat me like a princess, showering me with gifts all the time!"

This mostly emerges in the mother-daughter dynamic. You will often feel like she compares and competes with you. This is because of the insecurities and discontent she felt in her life. She might get jealous of your looks, your achievements, and how well you're going about life. Sometimes she would try to criticize you or sabotage your plans. A disturbing yet classic example of this is the mother that parades around in your old clothes, in public and despite the size parity, to demonstrate that she still has it and is just as sexy as her teenage/20-something daughter. Great, you managed to squeeze into my size 2 jeans, but your size 6 waistline is now squishing out over your belt.

- **Gas-Lighting**

I cannot even explain how severely this aspect of narcissism affects children. My mother made me feel like I was losing my mind all this time. Have you ever felt like blowing a gasket while in a confrontational argument with your mother? This term is defined as gas-lighting, which is generally defined as creating self-doubt by some method.

There are many aspects of gas-lighting, some of them could be:

- Being told you are exaggerating
- Being told "that's not what I said, you're misunderstood"
- Lying
- Making excuses
- Convincing that "it was just a joke"
- Disregarding your emotions

- Taunting about having memory issues "that's not how it happened"

- **Victim-Mentality**

Narcissists tend to love drama. How else would they seek attention? They only want to gain sympathy through their manipulation tactics. Have you ever made a decision in your life that didn't include your mother? Did she throw a tantrum about it and made it all about herself?
A narcissistic mother would usually start blaming herself and her upbringing. She will probably throw a grim story about how she felt singled out when you don't share something with her. No matter what kind of mental abuse she inflicts upon you, she will *always* be the victim.

- **Taking advantage of others**

A narcissist would go about any length to gain something from someone. Even if it involves invading your privacy. The only friends a narcissist has are the ones who provide benefits to them. Narcissistic mothers only have friends that can provide some sort of attention and service to them. These friendships are shallow and lack emotional depth. Does your mother have such a friend, who she only calls when she needs something?

"A child's shoulders were not built to bear the weight of their parent's choices."

– Toby Mac

Narcissistic parents never realize the mental abuse they inflict on their children, nor do they acknowledge it. Have you ever noticed feeling burnt out and drained around your mother? Do you have feelings of resentment towards your mother?

Most children who have encountered a toxic mother feel helpless, angry, and unloved. The reason why this happens is that a narcissistic mother is selfish, and she knows nothing beyond herself. A mother must be selfless when it comes to her children. When she is not, this results in children feeling apathetic most of the time. Other issues add to the preexisting trauma in children with narcissistic mothers. Some of them include:

- Substance abuse
- Identity crisis
- Low self-esteem
- Extreme behaviors
- People pleasing
- Codependent relationships
- Narcissistic traits

The parenting style of narcissistic mothers is unusual compared to healthy parenting. If you feel like you are judging your mother in a negative light just because she's your mother, you should reconsider. I am going to shed light on several parenting signs of a toxic mother that might help you identify if she's a narcissist. Some of them are as follows:

- **Liar! Liar!**

"I never did that, you are just sensitive, I don't remember it that way."

Have you ever heard her say that when you try to confront her? A narcissistic mother will always blame you for everything, and will constantly lie as well. She will make you doubt yourself. You will get stuck in the rabbit hole contemplating the scenario over and over again.

- **Selfish and Self-Centered:**

She will probably forget to attend to your needs but not her hair or Botox appointment. The world revolves around her and all she cares about is her selfish motives.

- **Score keeping:**

"I gave up my whole life for you, and you only care about yourself!"
"I'm so tired of doing everything for you."

These manipulation phrases will make you believe that you owe her something. Just because she gave birth to you doesn't mean she can control your life. A narcissistic mother will shame and guilt you for how she gave up her life for you. However, you must understand that this is never the case.

- **Questions your decisions:**

You won't be able to make decisions when you're around narcissistic mothers. They simply will not tolerate that. Even if you do manage to make one without informing her, get ready for the drama!

"You only did that to hurt me!"
"You're so ungrateful."

- **Self-obsessed:**

Oftentimes you will see narcissistic mothers caring less about others, catering only to their own needs. Narcissistic mothers are extremely conscious about their appearance, going out shopping every day and whatnot. They want to always look attractive and keep their sex-drive in check. They are heavily obsessed with sustaining their youth.

- **Find faults in your appearance:**

"You're gaining weight and won't be able to fit your new clothes soon."

"That's not the way to do it, but go ahead and try your way. Then you'll see I'm right."

She will denounce your appearance all the time. Finding faults in your clothes, hair, makeup and just about everything. She will always want you to appear the way she likes. This projection is part of her insecurities.

- **Breach of Privacy:**

A narcissistic mother wants to know everything about their child. You cannot hide anything from her or she'll probably punish you for that. If you are sitting in your room alone, doing something that does not include your mother, it will become problematic for her. Talking on the phone with a friend will prove disastrous if you will not inform her.

- **Favorite Children:**

"You should try being more like [another person]. They are so wonderful."

A narcissistic mother will make you fight for her love. Where she will pick a favorite child and constantly compare you with them, making you feel like a scapegoat. When you have done something wrong, you'll be presented with an example of a golden child. The child she loves the most. But this chosen child can be thrown off the pedestal whenever she wants, and she will probably pick another one. The golden child is the one that makes her look good, and the one who receives all the blame is the black sheep of the family.

- **Dumping Emotional Baggage:**

The main reason why children in a narcissistic dynamic grow faster is because of their parents' trauma dumping. A narcissistic mother tends to lean on their children's shoulders for emotional support. My mother used to share all her personal experiences with me. I was too young to understand anything at that age. I was not ready to acquire such sort of knowledge at that tender age. She considered me her friend and did not care much about the trauma she gave me. As a result, it felt like I grew up too fast. Most people thought of me as mature for that age. All I wanted was to save her, so I was all ears.

- **Physical Abuse:**

If a narcissistic mother finds no other way to control you, she might physically abuse you. This abuse is used to form a power dynamic. She will probably slap, hit or push you if you don't obey her.

"I'll give you something to really cry about!"

- **Shallow Relationships:**

Narcissists often see people only as manipulation tools. They tend to have unrealistic expectations from the people around them. Either they think highly about them or hate them, there is no in-between. People who are aware of narcissists do not attend to their selfish behavior. You will either see narcissistic people having lots of friends or none at all. It is challenging for people to get along with a narcissist.

- **Abandoned dreams:**

"When I was a kid, I would never have done that."

A narcissistic mother would always want you to live the life that she desired once. She will always expect you to fulfill the dreams she couldn't achieve for herself.

"I've always been good at this. I'm surprised you're not."
"I already accomplished that goal by your age. What's taking you so long?"

- **Unapologetic:**

Narcissists never feel sorry for anything they do. Even if they do, they are probably faking it. The way they say sorry will make you doubt yourself. You will wonder why you made them feel sorry in the first place. A narcissistic mother can create drama out of anything.

"I do so much for you, and you never show appreciation!"
" You're breaking my heart."
" I did this all for you, how could you think about me like that".

- **Passive-Aggressive:**

This act makes a person question their reality. You will not be able to make decisions in the presence of a narcissistic mother and will feel guilty all the time.

"I'm a better parent than you'll ever be."
"No offense, but your new relationship won't last."
"You should try my recipe. It's much better than yours."

- **Loves Gossip:**

You will often see a narcissistic mother gossip about other people. She is always interested to know what other people are doing and enjoys talking about their suffering. And then she will pretend as if nothing matters to her.

" Have you heard how her marriage got wrecked, she deserved this!
"But never mind, what does this have to do with me?"

- **Miserable:**

A narcissistic mother will never feel or act happy. She will find faults in everything. No matter how much she owns or how much she earns, a narcissistic mother will never be satisfied. She will feel miserable even if she has everything in this world.

"You know this car is good, but we should've bought the other one."
"The food here is good but have you seen the waiter staring at me?"

Nothing ever seems to be good enough for a narcissist. They are in constant search of something better.

- **Best friend:**

" I'm your best friend, you can share everything with me."
"That friend of yours, she really doesn't care about you. I think you should stop talking to her. Who wants a friend like her when I'm here?"

A narcissistic mother will not want you to seek help from other people, nor will she acknowledge it when you form new relations. She will act like she's the only friend you want and no one could compare to her loyalty. She will use your vulnerability against you, whenever she wants a reaction out of you. A narcissistic mother knows your weak spots so she will attack where it hurts the most. If she finds you confiding in other people for emotional support, she'll try to manipulate you to leave them. Most people dealing with narcissistic mothers have a hard time forming relationships.

- **Does she actually love you?**
Do you doubt the love your mother has for you?

"I'm the only person who could ever really love you."

A narcissistic mother tries to *love-bomb* you from time to time. However, her actions never seem to match her words. One day she might mistreat you and the other day you will be the most important person to her. A narcissistic mother might utter harsh phrases when you try to go against her opinion. She might tell you that she doesn't love you and apparently, you've been the reason behind all her problems.

Can you identify these traits and habits in your mother?

If you did, you might be having a lot of questions in your mind. You might be experiencing overwhelming emotions coming up to the surface. These feelings are natural, the confusion, the anger, and even the surprise you experience. You might make excuses to defend her behavior just because you love her. Regardless, you should realize that this was not the kind of treatment you deserved. It's uncomfortable to confront reality but the trauma you've undergone is nothing less unfortunate.

The good part about all of this is having awareness about a narcissist, and learning how to effectively manage your relationships. It is difficult building boundaries with them, especially if they are your parents. If you are focused on carving a better life and want to attain a healthier version of yourself, there is a lot more that needs to be excavated.

It's not easy understanding the psyche of a narcissist. No wonder why we feel like there is nothing we could do to reclaim our lost identity. We can heal our inner child at any point in time, only if we choose to.

"If you feel lost, disappointed, hesitant, or weak, return to yourself, to who you are, here and now and when you get there, you will discover yourself, like a lotus flower in full bloom, even in a muddy pond, beautiful and strong."

—Masaru Emoto

Chapter:3

Remedies And Resolutions

"When we meet and fall into the gravitational pull of a narcissist, we are entering a significant life lesson that involves learning how to create boundaries, self-respect, and resilience. Through trial and error (and a lot of pain), our connection with narcissists teaches us the necessary lessons we need to become mature empaths."

— Mateo Sol

There is a limit to your suffering. If you have recognized the patterns, indeed your mother is a narcissist. Living with a narcissist is extremely problematic. Children who are brought up by narcissistic parents lose their identities. They spend their lives hiding in the shadow of their parents.

"Often children feel unheard, unknown, and used by their narcissistic parents," says Kimberly Perlin, a licensed clinical social worker. It is very hard, perhaps impossible, to spot the signs of narcissism when you're young, but as soon as you stretch towards adulthood, everything becomes more evident. You can either choose to stay with a narcissistic mother, which is not recommended for your mental well-being, or you could break the shackles. There are many effective solutions that can be implemented to handle a narcissistic mother. Constant fights, communication problems, and expectations are the major dilemmas of a narcissistic relationship. You can change your course of action and the way you respond to avoid the manipulation of your mother.

Following are some strategies on how to deal with a narcissist:

- **Educating Yourself:**

The charming personality a narcissist has might make you want to dismiss the wicked side they possess. However, if you try to educate yourself about the signs of Narcissistic Personality Disorder, it will be easier to handle them. You'll be able to recognize the patterns and move forward with resilience. The first step is to accept that you can't change who they are, but the way you react can be counteracted. It'll be easier for you to set up rational expectations for the relationship. There are many ways you can educate yourself on this disorder which include browsing the internet, reading books, and visiting a therapist.

- **Self-Esteem:**

When you are in a narcissistic relationship, the most valuable aspect of your personality is completely shattered. Your self-esteem. The endless power struggle, unrealistic expectations, guilt-tripping, gaslighting, and manipulation tactics have the power to destroy the confidence of an individual. If you pay attention to building your self-esteem, coping with a narcissistic person will become less challenging. Engage in positive self-talk and consider opting for a healthy support system. Creating a new sense of self is challenging, nonetheless, it is possible.

- **Self-Advocacy:**

Speaking up for yourself is one crucial aspect when dealing with a narcissist. They can twist and turn your reality to suit theirs. You won't even realize where you started and how it ended. The control and authority of a narcissist make us want to shut ourselves down. The desire to express our needs feels like a lump in our throats. If you feel like someone steps over your boundaries from time to time, you might want to be assertive and clear about your expectations. Let them know how you feel about their behavior and speak up for how you want to be treated. Express yourself clearly and let them know that you will not tolerate anything less.

- **Protect your territory:**

Narcissists can be extremely persuasive. They won't leave you until they get something out of you. You will notice them crossing your boundaries consistently and they will never feel sorry about that. Making and expressing boundaries is different from executing them. If you want to obtain serious results stay persistent with your decisions.

- **Give yourself time:**

Staying calm in a narcissistic relationship is easier said than done. Their behavior is so irritating, that one might feel frustrated for prolonged periods of time. To stay calm, you should try to practice breathing exercises, yoga, or meditation, which will keep you grounded. Narcissists always want to get a reaction out of you so that they know they have the power to control your mood. If you are struggling with having an important conversation with a narcissist, try to center yourself to avoid unnecessary drama.

- **Supportive Relationships:**

When you have been in narcissistic dynamics all your life, you forget what healthy relationships feel like. You become so familiar with the toxicity; your vision becomes distorted. A narcissistic relationship is emotionally draining and unfulfilling. Try forming new healthy relationships that are fulfilling and make you feel happier. Friendships that make you feel your best self and do not drain your energy. Try to meet new people who support you instead of abandoning you.

- **Trusting actions not promises:**

Narcissists are never consistent about their actions. They may say they will act upon a certain matter but will forget the next minute. All they do is make superficial promises, which they are not good at keeping. Most of the time, the promises they make are the ones that are beneficial for them and not you. Usually, a narcissist has their eyes set on the prize and they do not want to work for it. They can manipulate others to get things sorted out for them, while they do nothing for others. It is recommended not to fall into this trap, instead, tell them that you will not act upon anything until they do. Do not obey their needs until they do the same. You will instantly realize how unreliable they are.

- **Professional help:**

People with NPD are prone to drugs as well as other mental and personality orders. A person might be having certain traits of narcissism, such as an inflated ego and a sense of entitlement, but that does not mean they are a full-blown narcissist. You must seek help from a professional if you feel like someone close to you is experiencing hardcore symptoms of NPD. If you are noticing and experiencing problematic harmful behavior from them, they probably need help.

- **What about you?**

The mental and physical anguish of bearing a narcissistic relationship is not something to be ignored. Anxiety, depression, and physical ailments are a result of endless trauma caused by a narcissist. If you feel like you are experiencing these issues, it is recommended you seek help from a counselor or a therapist. This is not something you can handle alone. Try discussing your issues with a healthy friend, or another support system, who you are comfortable with. Emotionally healthy people do not judge and criticize. They are responsive to the support you require and will help you in every possible way.

If you thought your mother was irritant in her youth, you were probably wrong. An elderly narcissistic mother is quite a handful. Instead of getting softer with the passing years, she will probably turn into an enchantress. Her expectations will rise to the sky. Whatever you provide the love, care, attention, and money, would not be enough for an elderly narcissistic mother. This results in excessive anger within you. You will have to come up with a well-thought strategy to deal with your mother's non-viable behavior. After all, you are not living just for your mother, you have a life as well.

How to handle a narcissistic elderly mother:
Have you ever felt like engaging in conversation with an elderly narcissistic mother is a big challenge for you? Well, there are a few reasons behind that. Try to understand that your mother is from a different generation. She had different values and a different level of comprehension. This is an added challenge to communicating with them about remediating this situation. Especially as they age, and require more assistance from family members. There are several methods to come to terms with a narcissistic mother. Some of them are listed below:

- **No-Contact Rule:**

This rule allows you to:

    a) Set boundaries with yourself.

    b) Puts you in control.

    c) Allows you to heal/recover/rebuild as needed.

    d) Allows you to forgive silently (or not) to create closure for the situation.

    e) Allows you to (perhaps) eventually decide on when/how you'll approach mom and family when the time is right for you.

    f) To avoid the perpetual and chronic effects of an NPD, this appears to be the most popular path forward.

"How can I get away when I feel too guilty to leave?"

If a relationship is taking a toll on your mental well-being, you must cut it down. There is no need to feel guilty about this just because she is your mother. Although NPD is a mental disorder it does not justify your mother's ill-treatment. It is very difficult to cut ties with your parents but when it's toxic and unbearable, it's time you decide. You deserve to be happy as well.

- **Self-love:**

When parents are not able to provide us with the love and affection we deserve, the meaning of love itself becomes altered. We forget what love feels like. Being conscious of your needs and putting yourself first is the first step toward self-love. Realizing your worth will make it easier to put your needs above a narcissistic parent. Taking care of your emotional and physical well-being should be prioritized above all toxic relationships.

- **Calling Out:**

Calling out a narcissistic mother is the most difficult situation you might encounter. Narcissists are defensive and can live in denial for their whole lives. If you try to educate your narcissistic mother on her behavior and this disorder, she will probably respond with:

"Who do you think you are?"

"You think you're smart?"

"How dare you question me?"

It is hard for a narcissist to take a grip on reality and accept their behavior. You can politely try to make her understand how this selfish behavior is affecting her children.

- **Avoid Arguments:**

Engaging in arguments with a narcissistic mother will not serve you any good. It is like adding fuel to a fire. She will not acknowledge the facts, nor will she take responsibility for her attitude. Narcissists are never wrong, at least that is what they think.

- **The Gray Rock Method:**

When you are showered with numerous insults and constant altercations, it becomes hard to not entertain a narcissist's drama. You will feel angry and frustrated but trying the gray rock technique can do wonders. How about you try going blank-faced when your narcissistic mother is arguing? She will wonder why you are not responding to the drama and will probably go quiet in some time. No response is the best response. When you do not react the way a narcissist expects, they will probably go insane. It is because a narcissist thinks they can control your mood and reactions but they certainly can't.

- **Reinforcing positivity:**

A narcissistic mother needs a supply of your energy all the time. The drama she fosters is because she craves the desired response from you. However, if you try to reinforce positive behavior, a narcissistic mother might get confused. Your positivity will make them wonder and the drama will soon be sizzled down.

Have you ever noticed your mother only feeling tired when she has to do something for you?

- **Dementia and Narcissism:**

Old age brings problems of its own. Dementia, coupled with narcissistic personality order is rather confusing and difficult to identify. The chances of having dementia rise with age and a person might not remember things as they happened. Because of dementia, people might develop traits correlated with narcissism. Memory problems may present themselves as a form of gaslighting, as the incidents that occurred have been altered by the brain. A narcissistic mother may start blaming you for other things because of her memory problems apart from the preexisting disorder. You must know that dementia is different from NPD, as there is a deterioration of physical health and loss of cognitive abilities in dementia. Your mother might forget her attention-seeking behavior as well. These are some signs of dementia to decipher the difference.

Dealing with narcissistic mothers is not easy. The emotional roller coaster never seems to stop and you keep on hoping that one day she will get better but she won't. Our beliefs are altered by our mother and self-doubt does not let us move forward in life. All the control she had over our life makes us think that we cannot take the reins back into our hands. But is that so? Not really. There is always a silver lining among all the chaos, only if we choose to see it. You might think that you have tried l the techniques and tactics but your mother is still the same. It is not easy wrapping your mind around a narcissistic mother's behavior and actions. She knows manipulation too well that anything can be altered to her and you will not even notice. But there are certain 'do's and don'ts which can help you regain your sanity. First, we need to understand the strategies that do not work and why!

What to Avoid:

- **Forcing Therapy**

There is no way a narcissistic mother will go for a therapy session. Do not try to insist on her going to a mental health professional, just because you're tired and frustrated. The reason why this will not work is that she loves finding fault in other people, either she'll blame you and play the victim or she'll make the therapist look like an idiot. Narcissists feel like they are superior to other people and are always right, so they never want to listen to anyone above them.

"The doctor called me a narcissist! But what does he know?"

Even if she manages to go to therapy against her will, she'll probably end up manipulating the therapist. Vulnerability is not something a narcissist prefers.

- **Disclosing your emotions**

Please don't. Has she ever cared about your feelings? Your mother has not consumed a wizard's potion anyways, so why would she? As tempting and therapeutic as it might sound, revealing your emotions to a narcissistic mother will go in vain. No matter how hurt, sad, or broken you feel, there is no need to write to her about this. Even if you try to communicate your feelings verbally, there is no way they will be affirmed by a narcissistic mother. She will either knit-pick your feelings and will use them against you or she'll probably act like a victim.

- **Blind to your perspective**

Arguing with a narcissistic mother will only get worse. Whenever you feel like you have had enough, you'll probably try to stick up for yourself. You will come up with different scenarios in your mind about the injustices inflicted on you and will try to confront her. But then what? She will probably backfire if she sees any kind of emotions or determination from your side. You will see her teary-eyed and acting like she is not even aware of what you're talking about.

"You think I'm a cruel mother? You'll know when you have kids of your own!"

A narcissistic mother is blind to your side of the story.

- **What if I am good to her?**

If you feel like being good and all happy in front of your narcissistic mother will change her, that is not the case. Because you have been programmed to cater to her needs from your childhood, getting out of this mindset becomes extremely difficult.

"Have you ever felt burnt out because you made extra efforts to make your mother happy? How did she treat you afterward?

No, that is not what you are going to do. Attempting to make your mother happy by being good and ignoring her poor behavior will only drain the life out of you. You will be waiting for her to change all your life, but won't get any positive outcome.

- **Others get worn out too**

You know you can't complain to a narcissistic mother, right? Instead, what you do is talk to people who cannot solve your problems. The build-up is so intense that we can resist sharing the cruel behavior of our mothers with other people. But if a narcissistic mother can't change, your conversations about her won't change either. This will become an endless loop. As a result, people listening to your issues will eventually get tired and that is when the despair settles in.

I know you have tried all these strategies and the outcome was the same every time. Right? Now let me tell you what works!! I know it is difficult not to give into a narcissistic mother's manipulation. Your mind and heart are always conflicted, wanting to react and say something brutal to your mother. But can you really? No. You love her, right? Why would you want to hurt a person you love? And what about a narcissistic mother, does she care enough to protect or validate your feelings? She does not, so all you need to understand is to stop hoping that she would change.

What about you? You can protect your sanity and peace. Do you want to know the number one strategy that works best against a narcissistic mother? Self-control. You heard me! I know, I know you have tried this one too, but how about you give it another shot, trying my method? Trust me it works!!!!!!

You see, if you try to control your reactions and responses towards her, she won't be able to gather the material she needs to manipulate or taunt you. If your communication with her is minimized, how will she be able to control you? Sounds good right? Works every time!

What is even more mind-boggling is that she will not ever be able to figure out what went wrong. You will achieve ultimate peace of mind once you convert this strategy into a daily habit. The results? No gas-lighting, love-bombing or manipulations will bother you. That is how indifferent you'll feel. Some other magical self-control strategies might improve your mental well-being. It is so tiring living with a narcissistic mother. *Sighs*

Strategies that work!

- **Revamping expectations**

A narcissistic mother always expects the same response and emotions from you right? How about you revamp the expectations she has from you and give them a makeover? Let's bamboozle the narcissists, shall we!! For example, if she expects you to call her back immediately, how about you take your time and call her when you feel like it. If she asks you to be home at a fixed time, do not obey her. Instead, make your schedule and shock her. How many days will she quarrel about this? One or two days? Then what? Expectations revamped Viola!

- **Concrete Intentions**

If you don't feel like doing something, you won't do it. No matter how hard your mother insists you on doing it, stay concrete with your intention. Once a narcissistic mother gets sight of this firmness in your behavior, she won't be able to force you into anything.

- **Emotional detachment**

The most crucial part of a narcissistic dynamic is detaching yourself from it. This detachment can be physical but most importantly it is emotional. I know your mother is important to you and of course, you are emotionally attached to her. But you will not be able to live peacefully if you aren't able to detach emotionally. You might be thinking about how to do this. Let me tell you, no matter what a narcissistic mother says or does to you, try to depersonalize yourself from it. Because whatever she says might be a projection of her own inner chaos. How about you focus on your mind, breath and say to yourself, this is not about me. You will feel nothing towards those harsh phrases uttered by your mother, for sure! Try it and thank me later.

- **Diverting criticisms**

The constant criticism you receive from s narcissistic mothers is never-ending. So how about you let her know that you don't want to listen to any and tell her how disinterested you are.

- **Forever the same**

I want you to stick this one thing in your mind, she is not going to change. Who *is* going to change is *you* and your perspective. I know most of us to live in the hope that one day our mothers will be like we see them, but there is just no way.

- **All grown up**

Are you going to sit around for your mother to approve your decisions or will you stand up and take responsibility for your life? Nobody wants to be controlled by a narcissistic mother. Of course, what happened in your childhood can't be forgotten but you can't carry it into the future. Otherwise, your future will become burdened as well. Accept your responsibility and make decisions for a better life. No need to get help from mom, you are a grown-up now.

- **The lessons**

When faced with harsh experiences, most of us tend to make up a negative story out of it and stick with it for all our lives. How about we change our perspective into something beneficial for us? Most Crucial situations bring major life lessons for us, only if we can realize them. Try to focus on the positive outcomes that come from a toxic narcissistic mother, how about you learn that you will not be anything like her! Burn the past and move on.

- **Dependency:**

If you and your narcissistic mother are living under the same roof and she's paying for your things, that is a problem. Try to be independent and earn for yourself, this will automatically free you from any obligations. Of course, this may be a slow process but worth it as well. You will not be listening to any more squabbles of your narcissistic mother. Bye, mother! I am off to earn my independence.

- **Taking care of your needs**

Instead of depending on your mother to support your emotional needs, it's better that you start prioritizing yourself now! Self-love is all that you want. The independence and satisfaction that follows will make you love yourself even more. Order a large pizza for yourself right now and treat yourself. You deserve all the love in this world.

I'm telling you, these strategies are worth it. Although it might take some time for you to adopt them but when you do. What a sigh of relief. Day after day, you will start noticing major differences within yourself. And you know what is the most important thing that you want? Some peace of mind! These methods will make you feel as light as a cloud.

I don't like to sugarcoat anything; I know that these strategies aren't enough to cope with the tremendous amount of trauma inflicted by a narcissistic mother. Healing from this trauma is a life-long journey. The most significant thing to keep in mind is that narcissists are not born but bred. I am sure this was as shocking to you as it was for me. As I discussed before, we all hold narcissistic tendencies, some are healthy others aren't.

If you have suffered at the hands of a narcissist, it's crucial to understand the impacts and the role of healing. Do you know what is likely to happen otherwise? History repeating itself yet another time, one more addition to the doomed world of narcissists!

"I wish that people would stop destroying other people just because they were once destroyed."

– Karen Salmansohn

Chapter:4
Is it time to Heal?

The most important question that might arise when you've identified your narcissism in your parents, would be...

"What if I am the same? What if I turn out to be just like them? What if...."

You know, from the bottom of your soul that you certainly do not want to be like them. As we know by now, narcissists are not born but made by parents who fail to provide proper guidance to their children. Teaching your children the right way of doing things rather than overvaluing them in their developmental stage, is a very significant aspect of breeding narcissism. According to a study released by the National Academy of Sciences, "When children are seen by their parents as being more special and more entitled than other children, they may internalize the view that they are superior individuals, a view that is at the core of narcissism. On the other hand, when children are being treated with warmth and appreciation, they are more likely to view themselves as valuable individuals, which signifies the core aspect of self-esteem."

If a parent is able to provide appreciation and acknowledgment in the ages of 7-12, when the sentiments are being developed in the children, rather than teaching them that they're above other children, this can be avoided, says Eddie Brummelman, a post-doctoral researcher at Holland's University. You might be wondering, is there anything to worry about? Not at all. Just because your parents are narcissists, doesn't mean you will be one as well. But there is something to keep in mind if you want to halt this process. If you are the child of narcissistic parents, it is more probable that you attract narcissistic relationships into your life. Have you noticed going in a circle with the same kinds of people and relationships? Strong infatuations and instant fallouts? Craving the love your parents failed to provide you, from abusive partners?

If you are aware of yourself, you will be able to recognize the problem immediately. The problem? You have not healed your inner child. You will experience the same kind of abuse over and over again until you choose to break the generational trauma.

How do I break the trauma bond I have to them?

You must understand that healing from the trauma and abuse given by narcissistic parents is important. Learning the lessons from your experiences is the first step toward healing. This is your sign to heal and choose a happy future for yourself. Ditch your abuser and find a healthy partner for yourself. After all, you deserve the love, care, and comfort that come from normal human relationships.

Healing from a Narcissistic Mother

"In my life, you are the sun that never fades and the moon that never wanes."

— Unknown

How beautiful does that sound? The relationship between a child and a mother is unexplainable. The most precious relationship of all. A mother is someone who has all the answers to your problems. Someone who can understand your emotions, without you uttering a single word. But that is not the case when it comes to narcissistic mothers.

In childhood, at a tender age, we tend to form certain notions regarding our mothers. Children are not able to make sense of most things, they break them down into simpler, more understandable, categories. A reasonable example of this can be when a child breaks down complex emotions into the good and the bad. If a mother is harsh or cruel, she will be listed in the bad category, while if she is providing the child with an adequate amount of love and care, she'll be a good mother. This causes a split, and it acts as a coping mechanism for the child.

A child is so fearful of abandonment from their mother, that they try to stick with the idea of a good mother. The split helps a child find a safe place to hide their complex emotions, which they are not able to process at such a young age. The more abusive a mother, the bigger the terror gets. A narcissistic mother tends to abuse the child mentally and emotionally. The situation worsens when this abuse takes a much more severe form. If she is unable to control a child mentally, she will physically attack them. Physical abuse can make a child extremely frightened so the child might stick only to the concept of a good mother.

Let me tell you how a healthy mother acts. She will fulfill your wants and needs within set, appropriate limitations in your childhood. She will try to guide you through your challenges and even when she can't, she will listen to what you have to say. This bonding with the child creates a healthy space to breathe. Eventually, the child will understand that the good and bad constructs they've created are of the same person, their mother. The child will accept both the good and bad aspects of their mother's personality. They will understand that their mother is only human, just like they are. Of Course, this awareness comes with maturity and passing years.

The fear of abandonment within the child will vanish like smoke as the child will recognize that they do not have to fight for their mother's love. They acknowledge the fact that their mother will not leave them no matter what happens. Their self-esteem will boost significantly. A healthy mother will not hover over her child all the time, telling them what to do. Instead, she will give them space to learn from their own experiences.

However, the tables turn when it comes to a narcissistic mother. The way she acts is brutal and selfish. She will only provide love and affection when it suits her or when the child is acting according to her expectation. Otherwise? God forbid, she will punish her children or shame them, regardless of how young you are. The fear of abandonment becomes so entrenched in a child that they have no choice but to obey their mother.

I know it sounds terrible, but relatable as well.

Do you remember a time when you feared the ruthlessness of your narcissistic mother, so you obeyed her out of fear? This person does.

"When I was about seven or eight years old, I was playing in the dining room, and I broke some expensive dishware that belonged to my mother. I was so terrified, shaking with fear that my mother would beat me. This isn't an exaggeration; I was extremely scared. I tried to hide the dishes I broke but she came into the room, hearing the noise, and I felt trapped. Like the walls were suffocating me. I stood still, trembling with panic. What happened afterward is something that stuck in my mind to this day. She physically abused me and continued to shame me for what was a mistake on my part. And after that, she just left the room, uncaring about her own child, whimpering in fear and pain. The only thought running around in my mind was that I needed to apologize to her. I wanted to make up for the damage I caused and felt

really uncertain if she would ever love me again.
Thinking about it now, I feel sorry for myself. I was so
young and clueless. This is not something a little girl
should have to experience."

So, what do you understand from this? The only reason a
child acts obediently toward their mother is that they do
not want to lose her love. As a result, a narcissistic mother
will continue abusing, shaming, and manipulating her
children. A child however will stay conflicted and split
with the idea of a good mother. The child will constantly
crave her mother's affection and will try to win her love all
the time. Always looking for a good mother when she does
not even exist. This is how children become hostages of
narcissistic mothers and are unable to get rid of them. The
abused child will only be focused on gaining their
mother's love and nothing more than that.

What happens if a child can understand a narcissistic
mother's cruelty? A narcissistic mother is very analytical
and always aware. And when you display the slightest
signs of pertaining awareness, along comes the shaming
and guilt-tripping! She will probably shower the child with
the appropriate amount of love and affection. Or should I
say love-bombing? This is a calculated move carried out

by a narcissistic mother so the child can fall into the trap of her being a good mother.

If a child tries to question the bad behavior, or distance themselves from her, she will guilt trip them for abandoning her. What a terrific game! The little child, unaware of these games, falls into the trap yet another time. And you know...This never stops. These games, these tactics, they go on forever if you let them. Until one day you decide to get out. These manipulation tactics of narcissistic mothers rob the children of a chance to heal.

The final blow is that a narcissistic mother will never be able to provide the love a child desperately seeks. The child will eventually become a puppet that pleases only their mother, feeling frustrated and isolated for their entire lives.
I can understand the overwhelming feelings that might arise, knowing all of this, but remember that you are not alone. You have a chance to heal and free yourself from a narcissistic dynamic.

"Healing may not be so much about getting better, as about letting go of everything that isn't

you – all of the expectations, all of the beliefs –
and becoming who you are."

– Rachel Naomi Remen

The revival of hope

You cannot bring back your childhood, and its lost dreams, however, there's always room for new dreams. Adulthood is already a difficult period of life, bringing with it all sorts of stress and anxieties. When paired with an unhealed inner child, the experience becomes dreadfully tough. There are many ways to heal your inner child, the first one is understanding the trauma and surrendering to reality.

The inner child can only be healed from a narcissistic mother when an adult can recognize the toxicity that still persists. It is hard for an adult to get rid of the concept of a good mother. So, what happens then and how to surrender?

Well, this is tough. The first thing you are going to do is to embody the idea of a good mother. Make yourself aware of the belief you once had of your mother. Think of how you wanted to experience the love and care from her. Then surrender to the truth that the perception you had of your mother was merely an illusion. But make sure to do this in the company of another person, preferably a professional. A female therapist.

Yes, it might sound hard and even overwhelming to open up to another person but the outcome is life-changing. You must understand that the love you craved from your narcissistic mother can never be achieved, but it can be relieved through another individual. Seeking help from a female therapist will allow you to experience the notion of the good mother you created for yourself. She will provide you with a comfortable environment to re-experience the trauma and begin the healing process. Remember that a therapist will not judge you for being vulnerable. The inner child will feel safe enough to open up to her, and the craving for an emotional connection will be subsided. An adult is conscious of the nonjudgmental behavior of the therapist and will experience the love of their mother through her. This connection with the therapist will allow the adult to grieve. Grieve the truth that there is no such thing as a good mother in their life and that this concept was merely a coping mechanism. It is not easy to get rid of a bad mother until you experience what it is like to have a good mother. After that, you can allow yourself to let go.

We all know it is easier said than done, but given that the adult will be provided with appropriate space and attention by the therapist to explore the inner child, it is very possible to heal. And as a result, the terrified inner child will slowly be able to see the therapist as a human, combined with the good and the flaws and a deeper understanding of their damaged narcissistic mother. The adult self will ultimately acknowledge the truth of the situation and will be able to regain control of their life. Your adult self will finally be able to bask in the glory of a newborn identity. An identity free from the reflection of the past, free from the cloud of darkness that your narcissistic mother had been overshadowing you.

The Road to Recovery

"Strength doesn't come from what you can do. It comes from overcoming the things you once thought you couldn't"

—Rikki Rogers

I appreciate you for coming this far. It is not easy to withstand narcissistic abuse. Living with narcissistic parents honestly feels like hell on earth. We truly are warriors and survivors. Therapy, of course, is the best way to heal your inner child, but do you know there are some other coping strategies as well?

Healing is a life-long process and it requires much resilience and persistence to finally set yourself free. Narcissistic abuse does not just destroy you, it destroys everything around you as well: your relationships, your perspective on life, your career and much more. These strategies might prove to be the stepping stones on your path to finding happiness. Shall we take a peek then? Some of these coping methods are as follows:

- **Setting yourself free from a Delusional Mindset**

I know that it is hard to let go of a narcissistic mother, but if you have already identified her as a narcissist, I think it's time you leave your fantasies behind. It has been a struggle for you but you will not be able to progress forward if you do not leave the hand that is holding you behind. The hand you have been holding only in your dreams. The reality? She did not even bother giving you the love you craved. There are some common fantasies that we form living under the roof of narcissistic parents. Some of them might look like:

"Maybe my mother will change someday."
"I hope they regret what they did to me."
"I'll make them realize the pain they gave me, by being better than them."
"I wish I could hurt them, the way they hurt me."

These fantasies might keep you bound with a narcissistic parent. Let's make this clear once and for all, narcissistic parents will never change nor will they accept the fact that they abused you. Do you know what you can do instead? Make yourself aware of these ideas and illusions you've established for your narcissistic parent and pull yourself out of the dreamland. *How* you might be wondering? Of course, this is not something to be done within a day, it takes much more time than we can imagine. Once you become conscious of these fantasies, embrace them, and remind yourself that there are things you cannot change. What you can change is your outlook and yourself. Be patient, we are in this together. With time and persistence, you will finally set yourself free.

- **Stop repressing! Grieve.**

I will share a friend's experience with you here.
"I was avoidant of my feelings and emotions for most of my life. I tried to bury them deep inside so I won't be able

to access the hurt inflicted by my narcissistic parents and others as well. Every Time I felt sensitive, I would instantly shut myself down. I tried to keep myself busy so I couldn't feel a thing. But this is not how it works. The emotions kept on piling up, which resulted in me having panic and anxiety attacks. I got triggered by every little thing. Ugh!" Then there came a day when I finally had to face my fears and pain. I realized that it was time to release in order to heal. My mental, as well as physical health, was deteriorating, and I could not take any more.

When you become aware of the illusions you've been living in, take your time and ponder over them. I suggest you don't hide away. Have an honest talk with yourself and grieve the fact that you are letting go of these delusions and pipe dreams. Grieving isn't easy. I believe it's the toughest part of the healing process. Give it time and try to be patient with yourself. Everybody has their way of grieving so there's no defined method to dissolve and process the pain. Some people listen to music, take long walks, and paint, while others might journal their emotions.

Find the way that suits you the best and try to incorporate it into your daily life.

This deep-rooted trauma might surface in the form of extreme sadness and anger as well. For the above person, it was both. The only way to avoid acting on these emotions is to write them down or feel them consciously. The grieving process takes time and is generally very uncomfortable. Allow yourself to have solo time so that you do not project your feelings onto other people.

You do not want to hurt anyone, right?

- **Lamenting the love you craved from your parents**

Who doesn't want loving and caring parents? If you did not get them, this is not your fault at all. Assuming you do not deserve love is a false notion that comes with the abuse caused by narcissistic parents.

You deserve all the love in this world, and you need to remember at all costs that you are lovable. Grieving the parents you never had, and the love you never received, is the basis of your healing process. How about you make up a list of what ideal parents look like, or the healthy parents you've witnessed in your life?

Compare them with the experience you have had with your parents, and grieve the unfulfilled expectations you had from them. Going through this list will probably bring about overwhelming feelings for you, but once the truth settles in, you'll be relieved from the false expectations.

- **Positive self-talk**

Do you feel insecure and triggered most of the time? If you have experienced these feelings, you should be aware that this can be a cause of abuse your narcissistic parents gave you. Narcissistic parents tend to trigger insecurities within us, which results in a negative attitude towards life in general. You will be surrounded by negative thoughts almost every day, in almost every area of your life, which creates hurdles in your path to progress.

The way you think about yourself matters a lot. If you are constantly stuck in the loop of negative self-talk, you will act accordingly. Trusting yourself would become difficult and self-doubt creeps in at all times.

However, if you learn to transform this negative self-talk into a positive one, you will start noticing major changes within yourself, and your environment. If your narcissistic parents weren't able to affirm most of your beliefs, you can! Some of the negative beliefs you might hold about yourself may look like:

"Do I even have it in me to heal from the trauma?"

How about you change this into a more positive and confident affirmation like,
"I have the potential to make my life better!"

How about you try to affirm this aloud,
"I love myself and I deserve all the love of this world!"
How does that feel? I hope that feels soothing and full of love!

- **Catching up with others**

The sense of isolation that comes with dealing with narcissistic parents is real. A narcissistic parent would never want you to have good friends as well as other intimate relationships. They would always cherry-pick flaws in your friends because they do not want you to stay close to others.

Also, have you noticed that, whenever you do form a relationship or friendship, it is either toxic or ends fairly early? It is because of the abuse our narcissistic parents gifted us with. We are not able to form healthy relationships nor can we ever fully trust someone. However, if you do want to work on this aspect of your life, you must try to reach out to others. If the old ones had been toxic, say bye to them and say hello to new experiences. Building healthy relationships takes time and effort. The foundations of a relationship/friendship should be strong enough to withstand any difficulties. But first, you might want to change your perspective into a positive one, and you should be open to welcoming the new. There are many ways you can connect to others on a deeper level such as:

- *Letting other people know you are interested in them by making them feel comfortable in your company. Ask questions! This will allow them to open up with you, without a hassle.*

- *How about you focus on the good stuff in a person and let them know that you like these qualities about them? This will make them so much happy, and connecting with them would be easier.*

- *The best way to connect with other people is through shared interests and experiences. If you have common activities and hobbies, you will be able to connect even more. Now that sounds fun!*

- *You want to be heard right? Others like this as well. This is the best way to connect to someone on an emotional level. Lend them an ear, and listen to all their problems and concerns. Make sure you do not offer extra advice. Just try to listen, relate, and empathize with the person. You will be learning more about your life if you listen to people around you.*
- *Always try to respect other people's boundaries if you want them to respect yours. Treat them like you want to be treated.*

- **The Altruistic Person**

Have you ever randomly come across people who help without expecting something in return? Don't you think they look so content and happy with their lives? I do feel that when I see such people. If you want to be truly happy, try doing something for someone without anticipating a return. Altruism is the act of giving freely, without feeling forced and expecting nothing in return. This is for your own happiness and fulfillment.

This act will do wonders for you! For most of our lives, we have done everything and anything to gain the approval of our narcissistic parents. With the expectation of getting something in return. It is because we have been programmed this way. Altruism will help you get rid of any kind of expectation, negative beliefs, and the need to get anything in return. Here are some ways you can cultivate altruism:

- *Teach someone*
- *Take care of someone*
- *Hold the door for someone in public.*
- *Help neighbors and friends with something they are struggling with*
- *Hug someone who needs it*
- *Listen to someone's issues*

Literally anything that makes you feel satisfied. Anything you like doing. Altruism can prove to be a form of self-care as well.

- **Mindfulness as your best companion**

The only way to stay happier these days is to stay in the present. The past is gone, and the future is yet to come, so how about we focus on what is already here? Meditation is the best mindful technique to keep yourself conscious of the things that are important. If you become aware of your emotions, it will be easier for you to process them. Mindfulness helps you take control of your emotions and it reduces stress and anxiety as well.

When it comes to dealing with narcissistic parents, this method will calm you down in an instant. There are a wide variety of mindful techniques which can be used to keep a person grounded, such as meditation, going for walks, and listening to music, etc. If you are mindful of your feelings, anything hurtful that comes out from a narcissistic parent will cease to hurt you.

I know that sounds unreal, but it isn't. The more you become present in the moment and accept things as they are, without the need to change them, you will notice manor changes within yourself. The things that bothered you about your narcissistic parents will not affect you anymore. You will surrender to *'what is'* rather than how *'it should have been.'* If you want to live a life with less stress, go for activities that promote mindfulness.

- **Being conscious of the narcissistic symptoms in you**

When we are the victim of narcissistic abuse by our parents, we are more prone to developing the same traits within ourselves. Because we are always in the company of our parents, most of their actions and behaviors are stored in our subconscious. We tend to play out the same character as our parents, without even realizing it. You must be aware of the narcissistic tendencies within yourself, especially if you get into the same kinds of relationships (usually toxic), and end up getting hurt every time. Make sure you are not self-absorbed. Acknowledge these traits and work on them so that you may have healthy relationships, unlike your parents. Some of these traits you should be mindful of include:

- *Attention seeking*
- *Need for validation*
- *Boasting about achievements*
- *Unaware of your, and others, boundaries*
- *Lack of empathy*
- *Taking advantage of others*
- *A sense of entitlement*
- *Selfishness*
- *People pleasing*

Make a note in your journal if you notice any of these traits lingering in the shadows of your personality and try to work on them so you can avoid being a narcissist yourself.

Why would you want to be one, right? It offers nothing but loneliness and misery.

There is no need to worry if some of these traits are present within you, it is not your fault at all. This was something passed down from our narcissistic parents, something we did not ask for. "I wish they gave us some love instead...oh well."

I know you can do it and you will conquer these challenges.

- **Recollecting your abandoned dreams**

I'm sure you had dreams of your own, things you wanted to do to know yourself better and to fulfill your desires, but all of this got lost in the control of a narcissistic parent. The amount of control they have over us transforms us into people who are not even aware of their identity. Did you recognize yourself before you came to know about the reality of your narcissistic parent? It is more likely that you won't be able to remember most of your childhood apart from the abuse.

However, if you are already here and want to heal yourself, give yourself time to embody your true self...a true sense of self, free from the notions created by a narcissistic parent.

After that, think about the things you liked doing or anything that you wanted to pursue. Go complete your favorite degree, buy things you always wanted, take care of yourself, paint, draw, sing, and do whatever fulfills your heart's desire. These things only remained untouched because of poor parenting and control. So, take control over your life as these dreams and aims will act as the stepping stones to your development and healing process.

There is no such area in our lives that might have survived the damage caused by a narcissistic parent. The psychological effects of abuse are devastating and everlasting if not addressed properly. A child requires an appropriate amount of love, admiration, appreciation, and positivity in the developmental stage of their life. All these aspects make up the foundation of a healthy being. However, if these basic needs of a child are being neglected by a narcissistic parent, the child will be left feeling insecure, apathetic, resentful, and alienated. The saddest part is that narcissistic parents are aware of what they are doing, yet they still cannot seem to improve themselves.

"Love doesn't die a natural death. Love has to be killed, either by neglect or narcissism."

— Frank Salvato

The impact of being abused by narcissistic parents is real and not something to be ignored. Most of them aren't evident, but some of them are, only if you search for them with full dedication. These effects manifest in the form of physical as well as mental damage. I believe the only people who want to step out from the arms of trauma are the ones who are willing to work on themselves. If you are aware of the consequences that arise from the abuse, you will probably let your heart grieve. And that is the only way you will ever be able to walk the path of true happiness and healing.

Are you still feeling unsure about the signs that might be presenting themselves?

Do you want to know the effects of having narcissistic parents and how you might be suffering in your day-to-day life?

Can we ever truly heal from this trauma, bred into our bones, by our caregivers?

Chapter:5
Will narcissistic abuse affect the rest of my life?

Who plays the most important role in shaping our lives?
Our parents!

The ideas, beliefs, and actions are taught to us by our
parents. Every parent wants the best of the best for their
children, but what if they are the ones who destroy our
entire being? The innocence of childhood, the carefree
and happy days, are spent in fear and isolation, if we are
under the supervision of narcissistic parents.

Long-lasting effects of having Narcissistic Parents

Do you blame yourself for all of this? Well, let me confess
something, I had this thought as well, where I was
constantly blaming myself for my parent's reckless
behavior. I used to feel like I was not worthy of their love
and I didn't deserve that either. My mental health got
worse with these overpowering thoughts until I started
reading about why I felt this way.

The knowledge I gained was a surprise for me at first, but
then it led me to the realization that I was not the reason

behind all of this suffering. My mother was a full-blown narcissist who made me question everything about myself. Depression had taken over me. I went into a regressive mental state and had suicidal thoughts as well. It felt like I had no strength inside me to bear my mother's hurtful behavior. The effects of her narcissistic behavior had impacted almost every area of my life, which I failed to identify, for a very long time. But when I did, I made sure to build up the courage to get on my feet again.

If you can relate to my experience, you must be aware of the consequences of toxic parenting that shatters your personality. Some of them are given below:

- **Self-Reproach**

Always blaming and shaming yourself for the love you didn't receive? Stop today!

This is a sign of narcissistic abuse. A narcissistic parent is always concerned about their own needs. Rather than being selfless towards their children, they neglect their needs and pay no attention. A narcissistic parent lacks the concept of emotionality and is not aware of how their children feel.

Emotionally sensitive children take this very seriously which results in low self-esteem. This lack of self-esteem takes a toll when you are faced with challenges in your day-to-day life. You will start blaming yourself for everything that goes wrong, even when it's not your fault. I know your narcissistic parent might have told you that you are the problem, but now you know who the problem is!

- **The yes-person**

Is it hard for you to say no to people? Would you do anything and everything, for them even if you do not feel like doing it? The shadow of your narcissistic parent is lurking over you, and the chances of you being a people pleaser are very high. Just like your narcissistic parent who is always focused on giving extraordinary care to maintain their image, you might be doing this as well.

What does this signify?

Narcissistic parents make their children feel that their needs are not important. When the same child grows into adulthood, they will be disregarding their own needs for the sake of others. Their own needs will feel like a burden rather than a priority, which indicates that you aren't aware of your self-worth. If you want to practice self-love you should consider your needs as a priority. Self-love is not being selfish. If anyone makes you feel this way make sure to say your good-byes right away. This is a red flag.

- **Emotional Vulnerability**

Have you felt like you have always held back your emotions? Were there times in your life when you wanted to say what you felt but could not? If words get stuck in your throat when trying to connect with someone emotionally, it is because of the emotional negligence of a narcissistic parent. Extroverted children tend to ignore emotional intimacy as a coping mechanism for their parent's narcissistic behavior. Such children build up the idea of others as not being reliable and trustworthy. They will not be able to open up emotionally with others and will probably form casual relationships that lack emotional depth.

However, the more sensitive, introverted people tend to provide extra care to others. They are more concerned about fulfilling other people's needs, and giving them love even if they feel empty inside. This is because they want others to relish in love and care, unlike themselves. The outcome of narcissistic parenting can be found in both extroverts and introverts.

- **Needy and clingy**

Because a narcissistic parent failed to take care of our needs, we might become accustomed to the impression that our needs do not matter. We might feel like we expect too much from our parents, which is not true at all.

Children who grow up feeling this way might become needy and clingy in their adulthood. They might start seeking extra attention from others, and form unrealistic expectations as well. If our parents did not satisfy our needs, others will mirror the same aspects until you have healed. No need to cling to other people for validation or attention if they do not give it to you. Try to stay comfortable with yourself and appreciate yourself first. This will help build up your self-esteem and you will start focusing on yourself more.

- **Echoism**

Have you had trouble expressing your needs to your parents?

Not being able to speak up in front of a narcissistic parent has a grave impact on the child. If you were a sensitive child, an empath, you might have noticed that whenever you tried to communicate your needs to a narcissistic parent, it never went well. Your parents would have expressed extreme anger, which is of course a sign that they are toxic. This impact of abuse carries on in our lives in such a way that we aren't able to self-advocate for ourselves. There are high chances of empaths becoming tolerant of narcissistic abuse in other relationships.

Are you able to speak up about your needs, or do you settle for less? Give this a thought.

- **Unhealthy attachment styles**

Another long-term effect of having toxic parents is getting into relationships that provide us with the same level of toxicity as we have already experienced.

Have you been in such relationships that make you question your worth?

This is because of the avoidant attachment style of a narcissistic parent, who failed to provide a safety net for you in the relationship. It is more likely that you are prone to falling in love with people who are just like your parents. The attachment styles are usually co-dependent, avoidant, and anxious, in such relationships. make sure you evaluate yourself, as well as the other person, so you do not find yourself getting attached to the wrong ones.

- **Developing Narcissistic Traits**

Well, it is what it is?

The absence of love and affection from your narcissistic parents might turn you into a narcissist as well. I know this sounds terrible but if you had a stubborn personality, coupled with the abuse from a narcissistic parent, it might give birth to narcissistic traits in you. When you feel undeserving of something, you might start feeling like you must do everything to achieve it. That sounds narcissistic, right? If you are mindful of your actions and intentions you can work on yourself to eliminate these traits. No need to worry! We all possess some narcissistic traits; some are healthy and others aren't.

- **C-PTSD and Mental disorders**

A narcissistic parent lacks emotional intelligence. They do not realize how their poor behavior has cost the happiness of their children. They keep on nudging their children for no reason at all. The chances of developing mental disorders are high when you are constantly being abused and traumatized. Some of the disorders include chronic depression, anxiety, and complex post-traumatic disorder.

Do you feel like you are always on the edge? Or do you always prepare yourself for the worst?

People who are subjected to trauma are more prone to being hyperactive, and they usually remain in fight or flight mode. They become emotionally numb and feel stressed at all times.

- **Self-isolation**

Are you in the habit of sabotaging your happiness? When a child is constantly reminded by their parents that they do not deserve love, they tend to isolate themselves. This happens because they are taught by their parents to not trust anyone, so the children start relying solely on themselves. As adults, we will avoid connecting with other people and will be dependent on ourselves.

As humans, we all need love and support from other people to feel content. If you feel like you can rely on yourself for the rest of your life, you cannot. This is called toxic independence, which will not help you in the long run. Let me remind you again, say it out loud, you deserve all the happiness in this world, you are loved and you are supported. Yes! That feels great.

- **Insecurities**

Narcissistic parents know exactly how to puppet their children. They are aware of the weaknesses of their children and will go to every possible length to hit where it hurts the most. The insulting remarks, the arguments, and the hate that they portray make a child believe all of it. This emotional abuse gives birth to a lot of insecurities in adulthood, which impacts emotional well-being on another level. In addition to that, this form of emotional abuse also leads to indecisiveness and self-doubt. The negativity of narcissistic parents destroys the identity of a child, which is further carried to the adult years.

These were all lies your parents told you! You are the best! Believe in yourself.

- **Self-defeating notions**

It's difficult for an adult to free themselves of the beliefs instilled in them by a narcissistic parent. When abused person tries to do something for themselves, they are surrounded by enormous amounts of self-defeating thoughts and negativity. This negativity by a narcissistic parent takes root and engraves itself so deeply in a child's mind that they fail to see themselves as any different, in their adult years.

- **Lack mindset**

Narcissists are always focused on their needs. However, their children, on the other hand, are forced to abandon their needs. The children of narcissistic parents fail to realize their needs and become avoidant towards them. If any kind of problem arises or a crisis hits, they might fall into extreme stress. They fear scarcity and need constant reassurance that everything will be better.

Try to take care of your needs, and prioritize them, so your fear of deficiency can be dissolved. The mental and emotional impacts are substantial and should be worked upon as soon as they are identified. It's a difficult journey to heal and, although you make peace with the majority of the trauma, it is never truly healed. Apart from the mental impacts of trauma caused by a narcissistic parent, the physical well-being of the abused person is also affected.

Do you ever feel like your parents' behavior has taken a toll on your health?

Effects of Chronic Narcissistic Abuse on Your Physical Health

Have you experienced uncomfortable physical symptoms growing up with a narcissistic parent?

If so, it is because of the trauma itself, which is deep-seated in our physical body.
Our physical health is directly linked to mental health. If our mental state is distorted, the physical effects will start becoming evident. You might not notice them yourself but people around you will.

Let us talk about how our physical health is damaged by narcissistic abuse. The American Psychological Association has mentioned a variety of negative effects that are caused due to stress. Some of them include:

- *Muscle tension*
- *Headaches*

- *Asthma attacks*
- *Rapid breathing leads to panic and anxiety attacks*
- *Cardiovascular problems*
- *Hypertension*
- *Inflammation of the circulatory system*
- *Higher cholesterol levels*
- *Increased epinephrine and cortisol levels*
- *Adrenal fatigue*
- *Insulin resistance*
- *Type 2 diabetes*
- *Heartburn*
- *Gastrointestinal discomfort*
- *Irritable bowel syndrome*
- *Erectile dysfunction*
- *Irregular, painful, or absent menstruation*
- *Increased menopausal hot flashes*
- *Decrease in sexual libido.*

Other mental problems can arise due to emotional abuse, including:
- *Memory loss*
- *Fear*
- *Anger*
- *PTSD (anger outbursts*

- *Terrified easily*
- *Negative thoughts*
- *Flashbacks*
- *CPTSD (chronic PTSD)*
- *Difficulty concentrating*
- *Moodiness*
- *Insomnia/Nightmares*
- *Racing heartbeat/Anxiety*
- *Multiple aches and pains*

If you are constantly leading your life in stress, you are more likely prone to some autoimmune diseases like:

- *Rheumatoid arthritis*
- *Lupus*
- *Diabetes type 1*
- *Celiac's disease*
- *Multiple sclerosis*
- *Crohn's disease*
- *Ulcerative colitis*
- *Hashimoto's thyroiditis*
- *Grave's disease*
- *Guillain-Barre*
- *Myasthenia gravis*
- *ALS*

- *Scleroderma*
- *Sjögren's*
- *Psoriasis*

The diseases I mentioned are not to make you uncomfortable in any way. But you must know how to protect your emotional well-being, so that your physical health stays intact. There is no need to worry, if you get a firm grasp, and control, over your life, there's nothing that can challenge your strength!

Have you identified the signs of being raised by a narcissistic mother?

Are you the daughter of a narcissistic mother?

The most damaging form of abuse that a person can ever experience is from a narcissistic mother. A narcissistic mother can be very cruel, to the point that you might think of yourself as someone insane. There are some specific traits that you can find only in a narcissistic mother. These traits might play out in your life in such a way that would be hard to recognize.

I know you have been wanting to get some answers regarding your mother for a long time, and I'm sure I can provide you with some. If you are the daughter of a narcissistic mother, you might have experienced extra brutal behavior. The psychological effects of emotional abuse are quite severe. The functioning in daily lives is influenced drastically for a traumatized daughter. If she isn't in the right state of mind, it'll become hard for her to experience healthy relationships. Raising their children would become challenging if they aren't aware of the traits they might be carrying.

If you want to heal the parts of you that are broken, you must be mindful of the dynamics shared with your mother. Let's explore the grave impacts of being raised by a narcissistic mother.

- **Jealousy**

Have you noticed your mother being jealous when you feel happy? Does she constantly compete with you?

Narcissistic mothers are extremely insecure because they could not achieve their dreams back in time. All the built-up frustration and rage are transferred onto the daughter.

You will see a narcissistic mother being jealous of almost everything you do. She will either criticize you for no reason, or will find fault in the way you look. Narcissistic mothers might treat their daughters like:

- *Body-shame their daughters because of her own insecurities*
- *Sees her daughter only as a threat,*
- *She will do anything to shatter their self-esteem.*
- *She lacks love and support.*
- *Fearful of their daughter's successes*
- *She will worry that her daughter will turn out to be more beautiful than her*

Narcissistic mothers surely know how to belittle and hurt their daughters.

- **Avoidant Attachment Style**

Have you experienced a relationship where you had difficulty trusting the other person?

The reason why the daughters of abusive mothers are unable to form healthy relationships is their attachment style. Narcissistic mothers usually think that showing love and affection to their daughters is a weakness. This results in the formation of fearful and avoidant attachment styles within the daughters. Such daughters will always question their relationships and will consider themselves unsafe all the time. Avoidant attachment style means when a person is shutting people out of their life because they cannot trust them. On the other hand, some daughters develop anxious attachment styles which refer to chasing love they did not receive in their childhood.

- **People pleasing**

You might have seen your mother pleasing other people even if she does not want to. A narcissistic mother does this to maintain her image so people cannot see the real side of her personality. A daughter might develop some people-pleasing tendencies, if she always spent time catering to her mother's needs in childhood. As a grown-up, you might start neglecting your needs for the sake of others which will eventually cause burnout. You will always feel like you are bothering other people when it comes to your needs but this isn't the right way to go about this problem. If everyone else requires love, care and attention do not you think you deserve this as well?

Don't you want to be supported emotionally just like other people you are trying to please?

Think about it! If you feel like you have been pleasing people in your life and you have not been getting anything in return it's time to reevaluate your actions.

- **Self-blaming becomes a habit!**

I can understand how you and I have been blamed by our narcissistic mother almost every day of our lives! A narcissistic mother would leave no chance to blame her children. She does not take responsibility for her actions and usually transfers everything onto her children.

"This happened because of you!"
"You did this!"

As a result, adults develop a habit of blaming themselves for everything. Even if they have not done anything wrong, an adult will still blame themselves for any disruption caused within their life or even around them. An adult may start believing that they do not deserve anything or anyone and will isolate themselves entirely. Well, let me tell you one important fact; it wasn't your fault back then and it isn't your fault now! We all are humans, we make mistakes! Try to get rid of this habit, if you want to live a happy life.

- **Turning into your mother**

Believe it or not the chances of you transforming into your narcissistic mother are real. You might start acting like her consciously or unconsciously only because you have spent all this time tolerating the abuse. Over longer periods it is likely possible that some narcissistic traits get embedded into our psyche without even us realizing it. If you notice certain narcissistic tendencies within yourself, it is time you regain control. The only thing you really have control over is your emotions, behavior, and actions. Make sure you are in tune with yourself so you do not walk over or abuse the people who are good to you, just like your narcissistic mother did.

The cost of being a good daughter is pretty big. There are so many things, so many aspects of yourself that you lose along the way, without even realizing. It almost feels like you have lost your identity in the endless loop of abuse. It takes great courage and strength to recognize your true self after you have healed the trauma bond created by your narcissistic mother. The best way to describe this feeling is...it feels as if you are born yet another time, a pure innocent child. But there are so many things you might want to know to reach this stage of a new you. A new you, free from the abuse, trauma, insecurities, guilts and whatnot. Let me remind you again, healing from this long-term abuse is surely no walk in the park. It takes resilience, patience and, most importantly, self-awareness to get through to the bright side.

How about you ask yourself this....
"What do you know about coping with trauma and abuse?"
"What were your coping mechanisms, growing up?"
"Are you aware of your coping mechanisms?"
"Are they healthy or unhealthy ones?"

Like I said, you need a lot of answers before you truly understand what exactly your narcissistic mother did to you.

"A bridge of silver wings stretches from the dead ashes of an unforgiving nightmare to the jeweled vision of a life started anew."
— Aberjhani

Chapter:6
What are your Coping Mechanisms?

Getting rid of a narcissist is a nerve-wrecking process. The mental grasp of a narcissist is so strong that it almost feels like a dog chasing its own tail. The more sense and awareness you gain about them, the stronger a narcissist resists and persists in letting you go. The love bombing, gaslighting, projections, guilt-tripping all of these manipulation tactics are used almost to an extreme just so you stay stuck in the narcissists trap.

Let me tell you something mind-boggling here. To protect their fragile sense of self, and their ego, a narcissist forms these coping mechanisms such as:

- *Love-bombing*
- *Gaslighting*
- *Deflection*
- *Projection*
- *Splitting*
- *Triangulation*
- *Distortion*

These are the unhealthy coping mechanisms that a narcissistic person might possess. So, on the other hand, to protect ourselves from the abuse of a narcissist, we form some coping mechanisms as well. These coping mechanisms can be either negative or positive. If we did not create these coping mechanisms for ourselves, surviving the abuse would have been extraordinarily challenging.

"Are you aware of your healthy and unhealthy behaviors?"

Have you ever noticed yourself acting a certain way when you know it is toxic and won't serve you well? No matter how hard you try to resist you fall into the hands of abuse. Do you attract the same kind of people in your life? If these sorts of questions are going through your mind all the time, you need to look deeper into what might be the cause of these repeated, difficult, circumstances. There are a variety of coping mechanisms and behavioral patterns that we develop, being a victim of narcissistic abuse. Some positive and others negative. Remember, narcissistic abuse is no joke, it takes a lifetime to heal the deep-rooted trauma. So, the coping mechanisms we create are, most of the time, negative.

If the experience itself is negative, the chances of developing unhealthy coping mechanisms is higher. But all in all, there is always a solution to revert a negative experience into something positive. There are a number of effective and healthy coping mechanisms that can be implemented to overshadow the not-so-healthy ones. But first, let me shed some light on the typical behaviors of Narcissistic abuse survivors.

"Do you identify yourself as a victim?"

If you feel like you attract same kind of people in your life, you might want to have a look at these behaviors/coping mechanisms. Here are some of them:

- **Always the Kind one**

The things that deprive us are the very things that we crave the most. Isn't it? We always want what we can't have, which is why the grass always seems greener on the other side. So, if we, as victims, have been deprived of the kindness of a narcissistic parent, crave this from other people. This craving comes at the cost of our own mental well-being.

"Do you feel like you're always ready to do everything and anything to achieve kindness from others?"

It might feel like you always have to be kind to other people no matter how hard they treat you. And the sense of reciprocity kicks in real quick as well. A narcissistic parent might have expected that you give something in return for the kindness they provide you with. So, your brain might be altered by a narcissist in such a way that you don't know how to receive real kindness. The kindness without reciprocity, where you do not have to give anything in return.

You don't have to be kind and generous if you don't feel like it. You do not have to do chores for others just so you receive the tiniest amount of kindness that doesn't even matter. You do not require an ego booster, in fact, all you want is real love and real kindness.

- **The problem fixer**

"Do you feel tired fixing other people and their problems as well?"

Because you have been a puppet all your life, made to cater to the needs of your narcissistic parent. It is possible that you are more tuned into other people's needs.

"Do you feel like changing people, and the negative aspects within them?"

A narcissist is always connected to the problem of others and immediately responds in order to achieve instant gratification. So, they might accustom you to the same behavior of fixing other people's issues. The most significant thing to keep in your mind is that you cannot change someone according to your own needs. And the other thing is that other people's problems are not your problem. Try to avoid involving yourself in such a situation as it might only harm your emotional well-being. The more you indulge in what is not yours, the more frequently you will be experiencing a burnout.

- **Blaming Yourself for everything**
"It must have been my fault!"
"I did something wrong."

Being accused and blamed by a narcissistic parent for things you did not do might create a negative mindset in the victim. They start blaming themselves when anything goes south. Even if it is nothing to do with you, you might still blame yourself for it.

If you are constantly blaming yourself for things that are not related to you, people might use this against you. Other people will feel like you are ready to take the responsibility for things that are not right and might put unnecessary blame on your already sore shoulders. They might start expecting you to make amends or find solutions to a problem, even if it has nothing to do with you.

- **Extraordinary Efforts**

A narcissistic parent never feels happy or satisfied with his actions, no matter how hard you try. You might try everything, come up with new ways to fulfill your parent's needs, but still get shunned. All these efforts and energy being put into the wrong person might drain the life out of you.

"Do you constantly find yourself putting extra efforts catering to other people's needs?"

"Relationships with narcissists are held in place by the hope of a 'someday better,' with little evidence to support it will ever arrive."

— *Ramani Durvasula*

Making others happy will become the most important thing in your life, just because your narcissistic parent has trained your brain this way. Saying no will become the most challenging word in your life and the wrong people will spot this weakness immediately. They will probably make you put extra energy and time into things, while the reward for this would be negligible compared to the task.

- **Unclear about boundaries**

If you are not aware of what is acceptable and what isn't, chances are you don't know about your boundaries. You might accept cruel behavior from people just because they think they can step over you. The self-esteem, confidence, and sense of self are destroyed by abuse by a narcissistic parent. So, standing up for yourself, saying no, and being aware of your own needs becomes a struggle for you. This happens because a narcissistic parent never allows a child to go against them or question their poor behavior. The child as an adult might tolerate all kinds of selfish behavior due to the toxic upbringing of a narcissistic parent. You do not want to make people use you for the wrong reasons. If you are aware of your boundaries, there is no way anyone could ever hurt you.

- **Drug Abuse**

The most common coping mechanism of a victim of narcissistic abuse is drugs. To hide away from the pain and trauma given by a narcissist, most people tend to lean into the soothing lap of drugs. The only place where they find comfort is drugs. They think that going numb will make all the problems fade away but the problem persists, growing larger and larger, the more they try to avoid it. However, Drug abuse is not the solution to the pain. Looking through your pain and making yourself aware of where it hurts might help you ease the suffering.

These are some of the examples of unhealthy behavioral patterns that you might have developed as a form of coping with the trauma. These behaviors damage the individual in every walk of life whether it be personal or social. If you feel like you have been struggling with these issues, you should try opting for healthier techniques to function in a better manner. We have already discussed some of the ways to deal with the abuse from a narcissistic parent, but I am going to dive deeper into more beneficial coping mechanisms for you. Some of them include:

- **Deep breathing**

Processing trauma is not easy. The overwhelming thoughts and emotions take over us like a storm. The anxiety and panic that comes when we are triggered is an addition to the pre-existing pain. However, if we try to practice some deep breathing exercises it is possible to process the difficult emotions. Whenever you feel like there is some kind of emotion you need to let out, try to inhale deeply. Take it all in, holding your breath for a little and exhale afterward. Breathe in and out... this will help you calm down a little, and will allow you some time to observe what you are feeling.

- **Journaling**

Because you have held back your thoughts, feelings, and emotions for so long, it is time to let it all out. If you feel like there is something you need to express about yourself or someone else, grab that journal instantly. When you scribble away your thoughts and feelings on paper, a sense of calm and relief will take over you like a warm blanket on a cold day. You will feel so light once it has all been penned down. Try to keep a track of how you are progressing in your healing journey by writing your feelings. Mention your fears, triggers, and problems to get rid of them. Make sure you take time to understand yourself and the depth of your emotions as well.

- **Finding new activities**

To help yourself give a break from difficult thoughts, try opting for a new activity. An activity that will keep you busy enough so your mind does not wander to negative thoughts. Some of these activities include:

- *Going for walks*
- *Listening to music*
- *Making art*
- *Painting*
- *Coloring*

Basically, anything that makes you feel good about yourself and is therapeutic to your mind and body. Healing trauma through these kinds of activities is helpful as most of these are an outlet for difficult emotions.

- **Exercising**

Working out can also prove to be beneficial for regulating emotions. There are many people who prefer to exercise whenever they feel frustrated, angry, and fed up. If you do not find some other way to let out your emotions, you should try exercising. The tension that is built up in your body will ease. The results of exercising are exceptional, as you will probably gain a lot of mental clarity once all the frustration is let out. You may find that it is difficult to breathe sometimes, in which case, I would recommend yoga and meditation as a means to relax your mind and focus on breathing. It will absolutely take some time, but they are surefire ways to heal physically and mentally over time. Moreover, a little exercise and a healthy diet will also likely boost your self-esteem too, which satiates the need for self-loathing, self-pity, and depression. There are numerous articles on this topic, which I will opt not to cover herewith.

- **Buying pets**

There are a number of studies that have shown that adopting a trained animal has a positive impact, at least in the short term, by helping people to manage PTSD-related depression and anxiety. Animals can help you cope with the trauma. Their presence is healing in its own way. Adopting a pet or a trained animal will help you in a lot of ways. Spending time with the pet will keep you busy, as well as affection, and love from an animal is always pure. Although animals cannot speak like us, they certainly can sense our feelings, and certainly don't mind listening to you drone on about your fears, concerns, future plans and other random thoughts that come up.

- **Self-care**

Taking care of yourself is a significant part of your healing. After all the years of narcissistic abuse, the mind and the body get severely affected. You need to take extra care of your diet because most people who experience narcissistic abuse tend to get extremely sensitive about their appearance. This is the result of body shaming done by a narcissistic parent, which ruptures an individual's self-esteem. Some people start eating too much while others starve themselves just to get the desired body according to the perception of someone else.

Sleep is an important part of self-care as well. The traumatic experiences and abuse oftentimes cause insomnia among the victims. The constant worry and stress disturb the sleep cycles for long periods of time which results in added anxiety. Make sure you sleep on time and if you experience insomnia, consider visiting a healthcare specialist. Anything that makes you feel better should be a part of your self-care routine.

Consider making a list of the things that soothe your mind and body. Afterward, start developing a healthy routine to implement these activities/hobbies to help you cope and recover. Watch some meditation or listen to music, create some art, or dance to your favorite song. Whatever makes you feel happy. Take care of your needs first, everything else comes later.

- **Break the Negative Thought Cycle**

You need to understand that whatever happened in your life was not your fault. If your parents were narcissistic, that does not mean it is something to do with you. But I can definitely relate to the constant blaming we do as victims. Yes, I know most of the time the thoughts that come to our mind are negative, and it is hard to clear them away, but hey, we can try!

The negative experiences should help us become a better version of ourselves, rather than bitter beings, just like our narcissistic parents. We can always replace negative thoughts with positive ones, with a lot of patience and understanding. Allowing ourselves to fully embody our thoughts and feelings can help us release them in a healthy way.

- **Keep the momentum**

Imagine how it would feel to put away all the emotional baggage you have been carrying for so many years. How does that make you feel? Free and independent right? How would you feel when you have embodied your authentic self? All of this is possible with a lot of persistence and hard work. I do not like to sugarcoat the reality; the healing takes time.

Healing is a process and it is not something that can be achieved overnight. You have to remember is that nothing is impossible and there is not defined time to start your healing journey. I know it is hard to forget what has been done to you but that does not mean you just sit there and watch your life fall apart. Taking control of your life is the most significant part, after the mental torture of a narcissistic parent. You see, if you are aware of your triggers, behaviors, actions, and habits, you will be able to see what needs to change. However, if you are not it is impossible to get out of the struggle.

Instead of putting your energy into a narcissistic parent, try focusing on yourself, to make your life better. If they were not able to provide you with a sound life, you have the ability to do it for yourself.

You wanna be free? Take charge today!

"Relationship with a narcissist in a nutshell: You will go from being the perfect love of their life to nothing you do is ever good enough. You will give everything and they will take it all and give you less and less in return. You will end up depleted, emotionally, mentally, spiritually, and probably financially, and then get blamed for it."
                                        – Bree Bonchay

It is widely quoted that it takes an average of seven attempts to leave an abusive relationship. Let me tell you something, it is not easy to leave a narcissistic relationship, especially if it is your parents. You go in spirals each time you think about exiting the relationship. The overwhelming emotions like guilt, fear, and shame rise to the extreme, just by the thought of leaving your parents behind.

Do you want to know why it is so hard to finally let go? Well, there are so many reasons behind this. Such as:

- **Idealizing and Devaluing**

So, what happens is that, when a narcissistic parent is busy abusing us with all kinds of tactics, we are unable to identify what is actually going on. It takes a lot of time to realize the abuse patterns. The reaction of an empath towards the silent treatment, coldness, and withdrawal is trying to please a narcissist. An empath will try to do everything to make a narcissist happy. And when nothing works and the empath decides to give up, a narcissist begins the idealization phase.

Now, this phase I am going to discuss here is something that you would have noticed. In this phase, a narcissist will act like their behavior is something you have created in your mind. Their behavior had never been that 'bad' and all you have been feeling and sensing is just an imagination. They will make you feel loved, they will pay full attention to your problems, and will act just as you want them to.

Do you know what happens after this?

You will start second-guessing yourself, for a narcissist's actions and will justify their behavior by making excuses in your head.

"Oh, they were just stressed and angry, maybe tired from work?"

No, it is not like that. As soon as you try to break free from a narcissist's trap, they will find a way to lure you right back in. You will think that everything has been settled and there is nothing to worry about for now, but along comes the devaluation phase.

So, a narcissist has changed for a while now, life should continue as normal. But the moment you 'think' everything is okay, is when the devaluation phase begins. The cycle of abuse will begin yet another time, and the normal time will become hell for you again.

These cycles will repeat for infinity, poor behavior, and then reconciliation. So, you'll try to walk on eggshells all over again just so you don't bruise a narcissistic parent's ego. You will make excuses for their behavior and will hide your true needs. These cycles will only confuse you and will make it harder for you to leave a narcissistic relationship.

- **Hoovering**

When you inform a narcissistic parent about leaving them, which is quite common when you have had enough, they will try all of their tactics just to get you back. This type of idealization is related to imminent abandonment also known as hoovering. This term means that, just so you do not leave, a narcissistic person will try their best tactics, whether it be physical or emotional, to keep you bound to them. All they want from you is to not leave them.

How else will they get their supply of attention otherwise?

"Narcissists struggle with being abandoned even more than most ordinary people, and they will do anything to avoid it."

So, what are the tactics that a narcissist will use in hoovering to lure you back, let's find out! Some of these manipulation tactics might look something like this:

1. If a narcissist senses that you are highly empathetic and sensitive, they will manipulate you by playing the victim. They will throw a pity party about how difficult their life has been, and they will probably shed some tears as well.

They will share all the challenges they have been facing like how badly their friends have been treating them, or it could be how hard they are working for all the family and whatnot. Everything that is sensitive for an empath is turned into an act by a narcissist, just so they do not leave. A narcissist will show how the only person that can help them is you. This is because they can sense the 'rescuer' personality of an empath. The rescuer is an empathetic individual who believes in giving unlimited chances, and has faith in the power of love. So, if you will feel the pain of a narcissist, you will try your best to save them no matter what. The guilt will take over you will waste all your precious emotions on this manipulation tactic! All you want is for the drama to be over, right? After all these efforts and attempts to give love, care, and affection to a narcissist you will probably empty your own tank. You will feel like a narcissist will be satisfied with all the help you have given but let me remind you again. That is not the case! You can never fix a narcissist!

2. The pity party did not work? Let us go for guilt-tripping now! So, you probably already knew this...but let me explain again. Standing up against

a narcissist or criticizing their actions is only going to harm you. A narcissist will always guilt trip you and make you feel like you are insane. They will boast about everything they have done for you and how you never seem to pay attention to anything. A narcissist will make you feel that you are ungrateful. Anything that triggers you, will be a part of this guilt-tripping tactic.

3. You really do not want to encounter the uglier side of a narcissist. When everything else fails, they will try to scare you with threats and even physical abuse. Yes, you heard me. A narcissist can go to every length just to destroy you and it will not even bother them one bit. They will blackmail, shame, or can publicly humiliate you as well. A narcissist might accuse you of something you have not done. Yes! This is how cruel and apathetic a narcissistic person can be! They can turn your life upside down if you try to leave them. These kinds of circumstances and behavior of a narcissist can be extremely terrifying for the victim. If you feel that your relationship has gone to this extreme, get out before it is too late.

"A relationship with a narcissist is extremely addictive. The cycles of idealization and devaluation, with the unpredictable, varying 'wins' plays havoc with your brain chemicals, causing what is known as 'trauma bonding'. You are, quite literally (from a neurochemical perspective) addicted to the narcissist."

Withdrawing from a narcissist is extremely difficult, it might feel like quitting a drug. However, if you are able to identify the problematic behaviors mentioned above within your narcissistic relationship, the leaving part becomes easier. When it comes to a narcissistic parent, the hurt felt by the victim is on another level. The feelings of a victim are so intense that it takes longer to understand what went wrong. There is a much significant part of your healing journey that you might not be aware of...it might be holding you back from fully recovering.

Ask yourself this...
"Have you forgiven your narcissistic parent?"
"Do you hold feelings of resentment against your narcissistic parent?"

Forgiveness. How difficult is it to forgive the people who hurt us the most? If you are struggling to forgive your narcissistic parent, let me tell you something...you are just an inch away from mental peace. Yes, easier said than done but if you really want to experience freedom, you need to understand the importance of letting go.

"It's not an easy journey, to get to a place where you forgive people. But it is such a powerful place, because it frees you."

—Tyler Perry

Chapter:7
Forgiveness–The Dissolver of Pain

Ann Landers once said, "Hanging onto resentment is letting someone you despise, live rent-free in your head."

That statement is quite profound and will evoke your mind immediately. Forgiving is the most difficult yet the most comforting part of your healing journey. Most people consider forgiving as accusing the other person for all the bad they have done, and then continuing on with life.

But do you really think forgiveness is that simple?
Not at all.

What about the pain, the hurt, the trauma, and the abuse which you hide somewhere deep in your heart? Can you really go about life just blaming the other person for what they did and doing nothing about what really bothers you? Will you forget how they treated you?

Forgiveness is not about letting the abuser know how their actions have hurt you. It is not about making excuses for their behavior and constantly blaming yourself for it.

Of course, after all the abuse received by a narcissistic person, we simply cannot imagine forgiving them. The feelings of anger and resentment are natural. Let me corroborate that for you. Letting go of these emotions is just as tough! So, what really is forgiveness?

Forgiveness is truly your peace of mind. It has nothing to do with the person who abused you, rather it is for the purification of your trauma. It is about letting go of all the negative emotions you might have for the abuser and realizing that the only thing that matters is your mental well-being.

You do not have to tell a narcissist that you have forgiven them. Forgiveness is solely for you; it is something that will free you from the burden of hurt.

Forgiveness is the awareness that you are starting with a clean slate and that nothing of the past will bother you anymore. Forgiveness is a form of self-love. Because if you truly love yourself, there is nothing that can hold you back from a healthy balanced life. No pettiness, no grudges!

Yes, forgiveness is very beautiful and healing but when it comes to forgiving our parents, this task becomes overwhelming. We can hold onto resentment as long as we can but eventually, we'll be the ones suffering, not the person who abused us. Holding onto resentment means we are somehow still stuck in the past and are unable to form a happy life for ourselves.

Forgiving is not something to be rushed either. We can surely put up a mask of forgiveness when we have not really forgiven the other person. Most people do this and the consequences are quite painful. What happens is that, when we put up a mask, we experience anger and frustration from time to time. Every little detail of our abuse triggers us in ways that are sometimes hard to handle.

So, what can we do to forgive a narcissistic parent?

You see, forgiveness comes naturally, and if you try to rush this process, it might be because you have not entirely understood the complexity of your trauma. Saying you have forgiven, someone and forgiving someone with your heart are two different things.

You need to fully acknowledge and accept the truth of the matter first...forgiveness comes after that.

What is the truth?

The truth is that your parents were not able to give you the love, care, and attention you once longed for and deserved as a child. They could not validate your emotions and were unable to provide the adequate guidance you needed from them. Understand that they are mentally unstable and it has nothing to do with you. I know it is hard to accept these realities but, to truly move on, you must try to do so. After you've acknowledged and accepted the reality, it is now time to let go of the expectations you once had of them. Letting go is not as easy as it sounds either, numerous overwhelming feelings will take over your mind. All your parent's actions, behavior, and words will be revived in your memory several times until it finally goes away. Let me tell you something, the meaning of forgiveness is different for each one of us. Have you heard most people saying, "*Just forgive and forget?*" Do you think it really works like that? No, it does not.

"Don't forget, ever"

— **Dr. Jonathan Marshall, PhD**

You can never forget the hurt anyone has caused you, the pain and suffering can be lessened but never really forgotten. I consider these hurts and pains as a part of our lessons. After all, if we are able to pull apart the good out of distressing situations, I think we've achieved a lot. Not everyone is able to turn their painful experiences into something graceful.

Forgiveness liberates the soul, it removes fear and that's why it's such a powerful weapon."
—Nelson Mandela.

Forgiveness becomes extremely difficult if we do not deal with the things that trigger us. So, find out what triggers you the most and make peace with the parts of the past that hurt you, so you can forgive and heal accordingly. There are many ways in which you can forgive your narcissistic parent. It takes time but with patience, all can be done. Some of the ways you can implement to forgive a parent and heal yourself are as follows:

- **Making peace with resentment**

Resentment is something that eats at our souls while we are still living. Can you imagine the damage it causes us every day? Thinking about the hurt, the pain, and the loss each day only means we are clinging to these destructive emotions. If we cling on for too long, the chances of recovery and living a life full of contentment are minimal. I want to share my point of view here and how I made peace with the pain my narcissistic mother caused me.

Speaking for a dear friend of mine:
"...first of all, let me make one thing clear, I haven't forgotten anything about my past, I remember it all, however, I can say for sure that it doesn't hurt anymore. I was a sensitive child and from what I remember from my childhood years, I took everything to the heart. Felt everything on a deeper level."

"Transformation without work and pain, without suffering, without a sense of loss, is just an illusion of true change."
– Wm. Paul Young

I felt the abuse that came from my mother with great emotion as well. I would spiral into the same thoughts for days...thinking only about her actions, her words, and how cruel she was to me. I am not going to stretch my story, let us fast forward to my adult years.

Yes, I held on to resentment for many years and did not even realize how negatively this had been impacting my life. My relationships were a mess, I had zero friends and my mental state was quite critical. I can't begin to explain how all areas of my life were deteriorating, and I was burning inside with rage, anger, and frustration.

And in my heart, I knew the reasons why I was this way, so I decided to educate myself and get the help I desperately needed to move forward in my life. My healing journey is still in process, but let's talk about the resentment part. The thing that destroyed so many precious years of my life.

As an empath, I decided to see my mother as human only. Humans are after all full of flaws and errors. Every human has the capacity to err, so why hold on to grudges and burn our own house down? This is not a justification for the abuse I suffered, this was just my way of realizing that we all are the same in one way or another.

My mother told me a lot of stuff about her life and what happened to her, which, of course, matured me at a very young age. I wasn't able to understand those things in my childhood but I replayed all those memories again *and again, and I was able to pick the right details. The details that made her 'that' way. A narcissist.*

I started to see the good and bad sides of her and accepted her the way she was, at least in my heart. And let me tell you about something really beautiful I experienced after this. Once I saw her as a human, and then my mother, all I had in my spirit was love for her. Love without expectation.

I hope my perspective reaches straight to your heart and letting go of resentment becomes easier for you. Try not to hold on to the bad side of your parents as it will only destroy your peace of mind.

- **Setting realistic expectations**

Expectations are natural. Let us talk about this from a realistic point of view. There are very few things in our life to which we do not attach strings to. Otherwise, most of the time, we expect reciprocation. Who does anything expecting something in return these days right?

Well, some people do. If you are living in the fantasy of unrealistic expectations, you might want to leave now. Expecting your narcissistic parent to apologize? Expecting them to change? Give you the love and care you deserve. That is not going to happen.

Sometimes we become so stubborn because of our narcissistic parents that we just cannot seem to lower our expectations. Accept the fact that your parents are who they are, and develop realistic expectations of them. It is okay if they weren't able to give you the love you wanted, you can love yourself. There are plenty of good people out there as well, they will love you with all their hearts! Trust the process.

- **Shedding light on the good side**

You know humans are not perfect. There is always a good side, and a bad one, in all of us. Even the ones who were lucky enough to receive affection and care from their parents would have witnessed some kind of flaw.

"Holding on to pain, anger, guilt or shame is the glue that binds us to the situation we want to escape."

– Iyanla Vanzant

I hope you know that there is no such parent in this world who can provide 'everything' to their children. I know it's not an easy job to accept the good side of your parents after all the harm they've caused you, but hey, you can give it a try. Try to see them as human as they are, and hold onto the good stuff. Over time you will eventually learn to let go of the bad memories and move on into a better life ahead.

- **Embracing individuality**

Let me remind you again that forgiveness does not mean you are denying what has been done to you by your narcissistic parent. It just means that you love yourself enough to heal the inner child that has been clinging to the parent for a long time.

You are a grown-up now and, as an adult, exploring the side of you that had been controlled and abused by a narcissistic parent is something you should look forward to.

A part of you that is separated from your child self who is holding on to the unrealistic expectation of love from their parents. You have the responsibility and are credible enough, to mold your life into whatever way you like. You are able to create the environment you craved in your childhood today, only if you wish to nurture your unique self.

"We are not meant to stay wounded. We are supposed to move through our tragedies and challenges and to help each other move through the many painful episodes of our lives. By remaining stuck in the power of our wounds, we block our own transformation. We overlook the greater gifts inherent in our wounds—the strengths to overcome them and the lessons that we are meant to receive through them. Wounds are the means through which we enter the hearts or other people. They are meant to teach us to become compassionate and wise."

— Caroline Myss

- **They still have a place in your heart**

After all your parents have done to you, you still love them, right? I know, I know the anger, frustration, and all those negative emotions are there, but there is always something good to remember. If you have accepted the reality, and are able to see your parents as human, you will start loving them back. You will be able to identify the parts of your parent's life where they suffered as well. Maybe they, too, did not receive the love they needed as children. That is why they behaved in a narcissistic, abusive, manner. Try to develop empathy for your parents as this will help you move on from the resentment and pain. Welcome your parents back into your heart with a newfound perspective.

- **The true commitment**

Forgiveness is a process. The years of abuse are extremely hard to process, looked at, and gulped in an instant. The longer the years of abuse, the harder it gets to heal. Staying committed to your healing journey is something that requires willpower and the flexibility to change. Rigidity and resistance to change will create even more problems that you will not be able to carry. You just want to release the burden of abuse and hurt you are carrying, rather than adding additional stress to it. If you want to heal yourself completely, you need to see eye to eye with reality. You need to understand the complexity of the situation and how it has affected you all these years. When you are focused on yourself and are giving full attention to establishing a better version of yourself, there is nothing that can come your way. Try to form healthy routines for yourself and commit to self-love. I guarantee that there will not be anything that will disrupt your inner peace once you start loving yourself.

"You may encounter many defeats, but you must not be defeated. In fact, it may be necessary to encounter the defeats, so you can know who you are, what you can rise from, and how you can still come out of it."

— Maya Angelou

Being patient with yourself is the key aspect of your healing journey. No need to rush anything, it all comes naturally. There will be times when you will feel like giving up, difficult emotions will surface and hurt you even more. However, the transformation process is a sight to behold. You will experience utter peace and a sense of relief once you get that weight of trauma off your shoulders. The journey might be rocky but the destination, beautiful.

Have you ever thought about what the healed version of yourself would look like?
What about your appearance?

Your emotional state?

I can try to give you a glimpse of what a happy and healthy person looks like. I am positive you would want to take a peek into the good stuff.

Chapter:8
A new you, A new life

The changes you make in your life are going to prove good if your intentions are pure. I know life has been tough for us due to the abuse, but hey, haven't we all learned a lot as well? If these experiences were not a part of our life, maybe we wouldn't have reached the place where we are today. Not everyone has the capacity, and the understanding, to learn from the pain. Most people tend to move in a circle all their lives, not learning from their mistakes and repeating the same things over and over again.

Have you ever thought about how far you've come in this life?

There are people who tend to give up when they are hurt and abused. Not everyone is able to make better choices for themselves. So, if you have been given a chance to improve your life, wait no more. You have the power to take control of your life and steer in the right direction. We do not get to choose our parents. There are many things in our lives that we cannot control. Such as other people's responses, their actions, and what they do to us.

Our narcissistic parents have taught us a lot, let's try to appreciate this truth.

Look where we have reached. Once you truly understand the real meaning of healing and why the trauma needs to be healed, you will develop a sense of commitment. A commitment towards yourself and your life.

"Abuse is never deserved, it is an exploitation of innocence."

– Lorraine Nilon

When a person has been abused for so long, they develop gears that are very difficult to conquer. When something starts going well in our life, we somehow fear that something will go wrong. And all this is based on the past only. But this isn't the case, it's just the fear that our narcissistic parents filled us up with. The wisdom we have gained all these years will make you understand why all had to happen this way.

No one's journey is easy. There are a number of obstacles here and there and that's just how life is. Nothing is perfect and setting realistic expectations from people, as well as in life, is something we all should look forward to.

As I said, there is no justification for the abuse that our narcissistic parents provided us with. But the power of decisions is in your hands if you wish to embody it.

Changes are always uncomfortable but they are the only thing that is constant. The world around us is always evolving, right? We should too!

So, have you ever imagined how it would feel like to have a new life? A life free from fear, guilt, and shame? A life full of happiness and positivity?

Starting a healthy life can be difficult for victims of abuse. They've been tortured for so long that they aren't able to see the brighter side of life. They are full of guilt, shame, anger, fear, and their self-esteem is shattered as well. Knowledge and wisdom itself are not enough for the victim to move through the hard phases of life. The implementation of these aspects is what really makes a difference. A healthy life means you are ready to accept and acknowledge the facts about your narcissistic parents and how they abused you. After the acknowledgment comes the part of acceptance. Accepting that some things are just out of our control and moving on.

"I am not what happened to me. I am what I choose to become."

— Carl Jung

When you make big lifestyle changes, especially if you have been abused, it will be overwhelming at first but worth it in the end. So, what does a healthy person look like?

If a person is struggling to let go of the past, and is unable to attend to hard feelings alone, they need to seek help. A professional therapist or a psychologist is required to help the victim heal their inner child. A therapist will guide them about their trigger points, the pain areas, and everything else that needs to be taken care of. They will handle the victim with absolute care and will listen to each and every detail with full attention. A therapist will also address efficient measures that the victim can take to distract their mind from constant overthinking. The help of a therapist is an added support to a victim's healing journey.

A person who wishes to make changes in their life will choose activities that benefit them emotionally as well as physically. The activities might include anything including coloring, cycling, creating art, and whatnot. Most victims of narcissistic abuse lack true friendships. I know there is a huge problem when it comes to trusting people as the victims start doubting the intentions of every other person. And it is okay to take as much time to get comfortable with a person before really jumping into full-fledged friendships/commitments.

Starting anew can be difficult as most people tend to worry that they will make the wrong decisions, especially the ones who are abused. They are unable to stand up for themselves as they have been under the negative/abusive influence of a narcissistic parent.

It will take time and effort to make a new life being a victim of abuse. There will be minor setbacks here and there but hey, that is a part of life. No need to worry about unnecessary drama, just focus on yourself and your mental well-being.

When you start loving all parts of yourself, even the broken ones, you will eventually get along with life in a healthy way. Taking care of your needs and prioritizing yourself before anyone else will make you realize your own worth. Making good decisions for your life will become easier if you are connected to your needs.

"The paradox of trauma is that it has both the power to destroy and the power to transform and resurrect."

— *Peter Levine*

You do not need anybody's validation for anything you do, like you did in the past. There is no narcissistic parent controlling your life now, all you have is you. However, if you are still living with a narcissistic parent, I have discussed many ways you can handle the behavior while still protecting your sanity. But remember, when you know your narcissistic parent's abuse is too much to handle, you should try opting for professional help.

There is no need to put up with your narcissistic parent and remember that you should not tolerate any kind of abuse. Try making new connections, focus on the dreams that were controlled by your narcissistic parent, do what you always wanted to do, just never stop. Let's never forget what happened, but try to move past the hurt and resentment, to build a happier life now!

Imagine achieving all the things you have always wanted. How good does that sound?

If you start taking care of your mental and physical well-being, you'll notice positive changes in and around your life. Exercising, as well as meditating, can actually help you clear your mind up if you're stuck in a rut. Let's recap some of the things you must do that can actually help you handle abuse and dissolve the deep-seated trauma easily:

- *Gathering knowledge about narcissism and narcissistic personality disorder.*
- *Identifying the patterns in your home.*
- *Applying effective methods to handle a narcissistic parent.*
- *Learning to remove yourself from the unnecessary drama.*
- *Creating healthy boundaries.*
- *Learning to say no.*
- *Standing up for yourself.*
- *Trusting and loving yourself more.*
- *Finding new healthy connections.*
- *Developing new habits and routines.*
- *Engaging in activities that make you happy.*
- *Practice positive affirmations.*
- *Identifying and resolving your triggers.*
- *Being able to work through your fears, guilt and shame.*

- *Letting go of resentment.*
- *Setting new realistic expectations.*
- *Making new achievable goals.*
- *Seeking professional help/therapy if you're experiencing C-PTSD.*
- *Focus on healing your inner child.*
- *Keeping yourself motivated.*
- *Trusting yourself, your decisions, and your actions.*
- *Making yourself aware of your own narcissistic tendencies.*
- *Never giving up.*
- *Embodying empathy.*
- *Building your self-esteem.*
- *Knowing that you are enough and you are lovable.*
- *Regaining control over your life.*
- *Unlocking a new version of yourself.*

I know life has been tough on us but if we focus on ourselves enough, we can surely make it better. The hell we have been through can be transformed into something beautiful.

Have you ever seen a butterfly before it actually becomes a butterfly?

The butterfly must go through many transitions, stays in the cocoon and is once a caterpillar. But the glow up is real. When the butterfly reaches its final stage of development, we can witness all the beauty and colors.

So, there is nothing in this life that can hold you back anymore and the power to regain control lies in your hands. Let the past be the history, that is no longer able to control you and your actions. Your narcissistic mother may exist in your life but, if you wish to implement the strategies I told you about, you can still save your sanity. But if you see that the abuse of a narcissistic mother is taking a toll on your mental and physical health, please make sure you consult professional help.

Always remember that your life is precious and there is nothing more important than this. Everything exists if you exist. This marks the end of bad times and times when you thought you could not do anything for yourself. Trust the process. If you can tolerate the bad stuff that has happened to you, have the capacity to welcome the new with open arms. It's going to be worth it, I can assure you that.

"Healing may not be so much about getting better, as about letting go of everything that isn't you – all the expectations, all of the beliefs – and becoming who you are."

– Rachel Naomi Remen

Conclusion

It would serve me great honor if my experience as well as my perspective reaches to the people who have been a victim of abuse. I really want to let you know that you are not alone and that there are others who are going through similar experiences as you. I hope that I have covered all sides of narcissistic personality disorder and narcissism in general. I suggest you identify the patterns of abuse and start working on them as soon as possible so you do not waste any more years of your life. Never give up on your dreams. You can do everything only if you choose to. I hope I served as help on your healing journey.

You have got all the strength inside you – you just need to dig deeper to find it. Once you understand the true meaning of healing, there is nothing that will come your way. Never ever forget to prioritize yourself and always take care of your needs first. Self-love is the most essential part to heal your inner child. Love yourself like no one else can and all the good will follow along without a doubt. It is time you let go of the wounded child that once craved the love of their parents. It is time for you to shine and make the best of your life. Good luck, with another person who experienced the same struggles as you.

Key Takeaways:

- **Definition and Kinds of Narcissism.**
- **Narcissistic personality disorder (NPD).**
- **PTSD AND C-PTSD.**
- **Traits of a narcissist.**
- **Signs of a narcissistic mother.**
- **How to handle a narcissistic mother.**
- **Strategies to cope with a narcissistic mother.**
- **Remedies and Resolutions.**
- **Effects and Impacts of abuse on victims.**
- **Forgiving your narcissistic parent.**
- **How to rebuild a new life.**

I hope you have the answers to the questions you have carried inside for so long. And all of this guidance will help you make the best decisions for your life. You are perfectly sane, ignore how your narcissistic mother once made you feel.

Take a deep breath in...

...and out...

...a sigh of relief.

Now that you have got all the tools, go out there, use them and make your life worth it. Cheers to the new life, the new you! Best of luck.

It was amazing sharing my knowledge with you!! If you enjoyed reading the book, please don't forget to leave a review on Amazon.

References

4 Long-Lasting Effects of Being Raised By Narcissistic Parents. (2018, October 18). Women Working.

19 Tips How To Deal With A Narcissistic Elderly Mother 2022. (2022, May 9). Coaching Online.

Adler, L. (2021, September 25). Coping With a Narcissistic Mother: 9 Tips to Heal the Damage. Toxic Ties.

Burgemeester, A. (2022, August 15). 21 Parenting Signs of a Narcissistic Mother. The Narcissistic Life.

Choosing Therapy. (2022, August 26). 7 Signs of a Narcissistic Mother & How to Cope.
Cohut, M., PhD. (2017, October 20). Five ways to cope with PTSD.

Corelli, C. (2022, September 16). Daughters of Narcissistic Mothers – What You Need to Know. Carla Corelli.

Fabrizio, K. (2022b, September 14). Strategies for Dealing With a Narcissistic Mother That Work. Daughters Rising.

Fabrizio, K. (2022, September 9). How to Deal with an Elderly Narcissistic Mother: 12 Tips To Save Your Sanity. Daughters Rising.

Ford, J. D. (2014, July 9). Complex PTSD, affect dysregulation, and borderline personality disorder - Borderline Personality Disorder and Emotion Dysregulation. BioMed Central.

Forgiving Your Parents. (2003, May 15). Oprah.com.

Healing From A Narcissistic Mother. (2016, December 22). How to Kill a Narcissist.

Healing From A Narcissistic Parent. (2022, September 9). – 7 Practical Strategies. Ineffable Living.

How a Diagnosis of Complex PTSD Differs From PTSD. (2022, August 8). Verywell Mind.

How To Leave A Narcissist And Stay "Gone". (n.d.).

How To Recover From Growing Up With A Narcissistic Parent. (2021, December 30). Annie Wright, LMFT.

Malone, T. (2020, January 15). Don't Forgive the Narcissist! Release yourself and let go of the hurt. Narcissist Abuse Support.

Narcissism: Symptoms and Signs. (2020, December 3). WebMD.

Narcissists: What to Do if Your Mother Is a Narcissist. (2021, April 19). WebMD.

Peer, M. (2022, July 7). 3 Ways To Heal and Deal With a Narcissistic Mother. Marisa Peer.

Perlin, K. (2021, November 5). How to Respond to Narcissistic Mother. Kimberly Perlin.

Robins, A. (2021, December 13). 10 Signs Your Mother is a Narcissist - Family & Kids. Medium.

Signs Of A Narcissist To Look Out For. (n.d.). HealthPrep.com

The 13 Traits of a Narcissist | Psychology Today. (n.d.).

There Are 3 Types of Narcissists—Here's How to Spot Each One. (2021, April 20). Health.

What Are 12 Signs of a Narcissist? 9 Traits, Diagnosis, Treatment. (2022, March 2). MedicineNet. (2022, September 9). Healing From A Narcissistic Parent – 7 Practical Strategies. Ineffable Living.

Made in the USA
Middletown, DE
31 July 2023

36005933R00106